T0039380

THE STORY OF
ST. JOHN'S COLLEGE, AGRA

THE STORY OF
ST. JOHN'S COLLEGE, AGRA

IPE M IPE & AGNES S IPE

PARTRIDGE
A Penguin Random House Company

To order additional copies of this book, contact
Partridge India
000 800 10062 62
orders.india@partridgepublishing.com

www.partridgepublishing.com/india

Contents

Acknowledgements

The attempt to write the story of St. John's from 1930 to 1999 was greatly influenced by one of our former Principals late Canon P. T. Chandi who has been a role model for many who came in contact with him. On two occasions, much after retirement, he brought up the topic and prompted to complete the story from where Rev. Haythornthwaite and Canon Sully left. At that time we felt daunted and totally ill-equipped to attempt anything like that. Dr. R. C. Sharma our former colleague and retired Prof. of History, Dr. Neville Smith an alumni and formerly Professor of English of R.B.S. College, Late Dr. David Livingstone our own alumni and staff who retired as Prof. of Bharatiar University Coimbatore (Tamilnadu) and Madras Christian College, Tambaram (Tamilnadu), late Mr. Neepesh Talukdar a distinguished alumni and formerly president of the Delhi Chapter of the St. John's College Alumni were all keen to see a project like this come to fruition and had offered help, if needed.

The most challenging task we felt was how to capture in words the powerful, yet humble and sacrificial nature of personalities involved in the building up of its past. We were afraid that the silent contributions of generations of students and staff will go un-reflected because of our inability, as we felt totally ill-equipped for the job, our apologies for the same.

We were heavily dependent on the contributions in the College Magazines of each year as there was recorded source or history of the College available elsewhere. The 'Principal's notes' of each year contain enormous amount of information and we are grateful to them for their silent contributions.

It is not possible for us to mention personally bands of student friends, from the play fields, class rooms, hostels, mountain treks, public life and also colleagues, senior, past and present, who enriched us with their friendship and fellowship. Their thoughts and counseling was with us all through the preparation of the manuscript. Many of them have completed their race and no more with us many are still at their race along with us, we are grateful to them, for their lives and friendships that enriched us and prompted us to complete this venture.

We are grateful to the current Chairman of the Governing Body of St. John's College Rt. Rev. Dr. P. P. Habil for his interest shown in bringing out this publication and present Principal of the College Dr. P. E. Joseph for support and facilities.

This project has come into fruition with the combined moral and financial support of our sons Andrew, his wife Aaakshee ; Nikhil, his wife Juhi; and our two Grand- sons Joy and Vihaan. Juhi has been helpful in the computer readying the script and Joy in transferring portion from laptop to the desk top computer.

Mr. Sailesh Kumar spent long hours with us in putting the script into book form.

Preface

Blessings of God Almighty enabled us to be a part of this great Institution, St. John's College, Agra, for more than half a century since 1956. During this long stay, initially as a students then as members of the staff, we got the opportunity to be closely associated with successive Principals, Canon Dr. P. T. Chandi, Dr. P. I. Itteyerah, Rev. Dr. S. C. Banwar, Prof. G. M. Ram, and Dr. M. S. Renick. The chance of being associated with a stream of distinguished students who are contributing their might fearlessly to the life of our nation outside the arena of College walls is the most cherished blessing we can recall. This book is dedicated to all, irrespective of religion, caste or creed, whose sacrificial lives and services enabled St. John's College to be what it is at the end of the twentieth century.

The suggestion to record and update the history of the College from 1930 onwards was made by former Principal Canon P. T. Chandi on his last visit to the College in 1990. He also shared with us the fact that he has made this suggestion also to few others associated with the College. Two decades have passed since then, during which we lost many valued St. Johnians to history. Urgency was felt to record the events of the period as it is becoming more and more difficult to recall and share the events due to the diminishing number of people left to share it with. The book

"History of St. John's College, Agra" by two distinguished Principals, Rev. John Parker Haythornthwaite and Canon T. D. Sully published in 1932 records the events up to the year 1930. This publication is currently unavailable and out of print since long.

Also it is felt that the very relevance of St. John's College to the city of Agra and the country is diminishing as years go by. Corrective steps are required to reverse the trend and that can be understood and formulated only if you look back into its history.

The present publication is an attempt to tell the story of the College from year1930 to the end of the century. This publication in no way can be claimed or treated as a true sequel to the existing publication as the events of the period are treated corresponding to the period of respective Principals, which made it more individual oriented, without intention, and apologies for the same.

A few photographs of the College of its early years' already published and available in public domain are being reused to give continuity and is acknowledged herewith gratitude. College Magazines of the years passed by provided a treasure of information specially the Principals' notes of each year. Chapters 4 to 9 deals with events that cannot be attributed belonging the period of any particular Principal.

Ipe M.Ipe
Agnes S Ipe

The Rev. Thomas Valpy French: Ist Principal

Introduction

Introduction

History of St. John's College, Agra from its year of establishment in 1850 to 1930 has been published as a composite book by two of it's illustrious past Principals, late Dr. J. P. Haythornthwaite and late Canon T. D. Sully. This book "The History of St. John's College Agra" is a well re-searched and factually correct publication dealing with its history of a tumultuous period. The authors of the present volume dealing with its history from the year 1930 to 2000 are closely associated with the College life as students, researchers, members of the teaching staff, members of its Governing body and also served in various administrative positions in the College for many years. There was a nagging inner urge and wish to bring out a publication to cover its history from the year 1930 on wards as we felt that old linkages and values are fast changing and future generations may find it difficult to understand the evolution of the policies and structural changes the College has undergone during this period.

The objective and purpose of the founders of the College could be clearly understood from the words of the following prayer offered at the time work started on the new building almost a century ago *"that its foundation may be laid in truth*

1

and righteousness: that beauty and reverence may be built into its walls, and so long as one stone remains upon another it may ever stand for all things that are pure and lovely and of good report'.(St. John's College, Agra- Its History, Activities, and Aims-1924). How relevant this prayer even after a hundred years, history of the past hundred years is the true witness.

We, the authors, very well realise our limitations and feel it will be practically impossible and beyond our ability to bring it out as a true sequel and in the format of the existing 'History of St. John's College'. Nevertheless, we feel it very essential to bring out a publication, as composite as possible of the period from the year 1930 to 1999. The educational, administrative and political scenario of the country has undergone rapid and drastic changes which make it difficult for anyone to understand many of the decisions taken and the underlying philosophy behind those.

The period we are attempting to cover include two overlapping watershed periods, -first politically significant the pre independence and world war- II period-, and the second immediate post independence period significant in view of nation building role fallen upon the generation of students and staff as a result of independence gained. The shape the institution has attained in this period is more influenced by the sacrificial nature of the community and the institutional leaders and less by commercial considerations. It covers a period under the stewardship of Principals and community leaders whose ability and vision leaves an indelible mark in its structure till the end of the century.

Administrative Frame work

The evolution of its present day administrative framework needs to be understood also in the background of the changes undergone by the Church. A student of its' history also needs to understand the linkages and the evolution of the Church of North India and the Agra Diocese from the days of Church Missionary Society and the Anglican Church in pre independence period to the present day as the College during this period evolved as a prominent a minority institution of the country administered by Governing Body and St. John's College Society under the Agra Diocese of the Church of North India.

The administrative pattern evolved by the College through years and the special rights and status it has gained as a minority institution post independence has given the Principals and the Governing Body much more freedom and autonomy in functioning compared to the contemporary institutions even the ones managed by the Government. They enjoyed much more freedom in functioning conjoined with responsibility and hence could play a more pivotal role in the formation of its history. The governmental role in their functioning was considerably limited as they enjoyed more freedom in staff selection and other administrative matters. Thus we find it easier to tell its story linked to the administrative period of successive Principals though the approach makes more vulnerable to become individualistic rather institution centered. We have tried to narrate the story revolving around the Principals, Staff, Students, Alumni and important visitors of the College and important events during the administrative period of a particular Principal.

Anglican Church,-Church Missionary Society,-Church of North India (CNI)

It is also essential to understand the linkages and changes that have undergone by the Church Missionary Society of England (CMS)- the founding society, the Anglican Church and the Church of North India (CNI) since its formation on 29th November, 1970 and the Dioceses of Lucknow, with head- quarters at Allahabad and there after the Diocese of Agra, headquartered in Agra since its formation in 1976. The presiding Bishop of the period of the respective Diocese remained the head of the Governing Body at all times and thus through him the Church had a key role to play in its history especially regarding the evolution of administrative policies of a particular period. The property, land and the buildings, vested originally with the CMS (Church Missionary Society) was administered through a Trust, Indian Church Trustees (ICT) with headquarters at Calcutta under the supervisory umbrella of the Metropolitan of India at Calcutta and there after transferred through the Church of North India Trust Association (CNITA) when it was formed with the formation of CNI. Power of Attorney, for all practical purposes, vest with the Bishop of Agra, President of the Agra Diocesan Trust Association. (ADTA)

St. John's College Society, a registered Society under the Societies Act forms the Governing Body of the College for all administrative purposes. It is formed keeping in mind the Government Regulations of the time and above all maintaining the Minority Rights enjoyed by the College as a recognised Minority Institution.

Chapter 1

The Beginning:

The idea of St. John's College came up to the C.M.S. Committee (Church Missionary Society) of Agra in the 1840s' even though already one educational Institution-Government College (Agra College) existed in Agra since 1823, established in accordance with a bequest made to the East India Company in 1818 by Pandit Ganga Dhar Shastri. The local C.M.S Committee began to conceive the idea that it is highly desirable that a large center of population like Agra, which was also a seat of the Government (North West Province of India) in those days, there should be a mission College for higher education of the 'sons of Indian Officials in the Government and influential classes of the Indian society generally' (Davies, 1832). At this time institutions of higher education were very few in north India.

The expectation at the time of its establishment was that 'this College would become the center of strong influence which would *do much to purify public morals, and raise the general moral tone of the educated classes through out the Province'*.

The Old Building of the College Built in 1850

Mr. James Thomason, the then Lt. Governor was the chief inspirer, and he along with a group of people raised Rs. 50,000-00 locally and the London C. M. S. Committee contributed an equal amount Rs. 50,000-00 from its Jubilee Fund in 1849 for the purpose.

The Rev. Thomas Valpy French, a distinguished Fellow of University College, Oxford, was appointed as Principal on 16th April,1850 and Rev. Edward Craig Stuart appointed as Vice-Principal a month later.

Both of them Principal and Vice-Principal, sailed together, by sea route non-stop to India in a vessel named 'Queen' and arrived at Calcutta on 2nd January, 1851 and in Agra on 13th February, 1851.

The construction of the building of the College was begun in 1850 before the arrival of the Principal and Vice-Principal at Agra. It was built in Gothic style and the designs were prepared by Major Kittoe, R.E., a member of the Agra Missionary Association.

The opening ceremony took place on the 16th December, 1852, by prayers offered by the Principal French in the presence of a distinguished gathering.

Early Days:

No system of University Education had been introduced into India at this time and the Principal and the staff had the responsibility of forming their own curricula and conducting examinations. Principals' report 1855 mention English (essays, translations and comprehension), History, Geometry and Algebra forming part of the course. In 1856 there were 300 students enrolled.

A feature that needs to be mentioned is the functioning at this time of Feeder Schools or Branch Schools attached to the College. Six such Schools are mentioned with considerable strength as: Belanganj- 100; Chatterghat- 50; Lohamandi- 125; Nai-ki Mandi- 30; Rajpur- 40; and Isaitolah- 30.

The New Building: A Necessity for Expansion

The first 10 years of the 19th century the number of students in the institution more than doubled. The total number that was being handled was: College Students 260, Boys in the High School 830, and 450 more in the branch schools. The Principal increasingly realised the unwieldy character of the institution. Number of staff too increased considerably from 12 in 1900 to 19 in 1910. The need for separation of the school from the College was suggested in previous inspection panel reports too and that it became a necessity by now. The arrival of Messrs. Arthur W. Davies and P. F. Holland in 1908 and Dr. Garfield Williams in 1910 gave more room for then Principal Haythornthwaite to plan and execute expansion possibilities. A new College building, Hostels and the laboratories on a site by the Drummond Road (present MG Road) was the wish and vision of the past Principals especially Mr. J. P. Haythornthwaite and Dr. H. B. Durrant. A new Hostel building 'The New Hindu Hostel'(Haythornthwaite Wing of present Haileybury House-currently Staff Room) was built and made functional at this site by 1909.

The vision of the new College building was transformed into reality mainly by the efforts, initiative and even finances of Canon A. W. Davies who took over as Principal in 1913.

Canon Dr. A. W. Davies: Principal 1913-1928
First Vice-Chancellor of Agra University

At the New Campus

Arts classes of the College were transferred to the new class rooms of the new building before the end of 1913 while the work was still going on the College Hall and the laboratories.

The majestic new building was completed, except the present administrative wing, was opened by the then Viceroy Lord Hardinge on the 9th of January 1914.

As detailed narrative of the happenings from 1850 to 1930 is available in the *'History of St. John's College'*, the book compiled by J. P. Haythornthwaite and revised and completed by Canon T. D. Sully, two past principals of the College published in 1932.

J. P. Haythornthwaite: Principal 1890-1911

Commission on Christian Higher Education In India and Agra Conference

An influential conference of indian christian and missionary educators, was held at Agra in February 1929 and in which a large majority of leading Christian Colleges in India participated. A suggestion to form a Commission on the Christian Higher Education in India was made in the form of a resolution by the conference and the suggestion was placed before the Executive Committee of the National Christian Council and after its acceptance by Missionary Societies Great Britain and Ireland. As a result a high powered Committee was formed to review the functioning of the Christian Institutions in India.

The Committee constituted the following:

> D. Lindsay, as Chairman, Master of Balliol College, Oxford

> Mr. S. N. Mukerji, Principal St. Stephen's College, Delhi

> Mr. S. K. Dutta World Y.M.C.A in Geneva

> Dr. A. W. Davies Rep. Of Conference of British Missionary Societies, Formerly Principal of St. John's College and First Vice-Chancellor of Agra University

> Dr. Nicol Macnicol, Rep. Church of Scotland and Secretary, National Christian Council

> W. Adams Brown – Rep. Of Foreign Missions Conference, U.S.A

> Mr. William Hutchins, President, Berea College, State of Kentucky

> Dr. Oscar Buck- as Secretary, Drew University New Jersey

The Aims and objectives given to the Committee were:

1. To Review the field of service open to the Christian Colleges under present conditions in India

2. To suggest methods for avoiding duplication of work
3. To consider how needs of the Christian College could be presented in Britain and America

It is essential to understand the resolutions of Agra Conference and how these influenced the development of the College.

> *'This conference recognizes that in view of the rapid changes taking place in India and of the strength of the new factors that are at work, it would be disastrous folly if the leaders of Indian Church neglected to take stock of the situation and to reconsider both their methods and distribution of their force.*
>
> *'Never has India had greater need of that ability to discern between wise and dangerous leadership which only sound education can impart.'*
>
> *'Yet while in this way the opportunity of the Christian educationist is enhanced, he has also new handicaps to overcome in the form of more competition to face and more government controls in functioning and also increase in the expensiveness of Education.'*

The Commission also made recommendations on individual colleges and it is essential to know these recommendations regarding St. John's College to understand the administrative and structural changes that it had undergone later. I quote some of them here as below:

'We consider the College should continue to render the special service for which it is qualified in the following directions:

1. *Continue to provide an education for Christian students, especially those of Anglican Church and Anglo-Indians.*

2. *Provide facilities for Christian students from other Colleges to undertake postgraduate work, especially in Science*

3. *With regard to work in higher sciences we advise the college to keep in close touch with the Foreman Christian College, Lahore in order that the work undertaken by the two colleges are complimentary. It should be possible to provide in one or the other of these colleges facilities for the training of Christian students in all the higher branches of Science with the view of them becoming teachers in other Christian Colleges.*

4. *In opening classes to women students, especially Hindu and Muslim women in co-educational lines*

5. *The practice of segregating Christian students in a special hostel be discontinued*

6. *The present Christian Hostel with the adjacent bungalow be made available for the use of women students.*

7. *As there is no particular significance in the development of Commerce classes in a city like Agra steps should be taken to close the Commerce Faculty and concentrate resources on arts and science.*

8. *Take steps to reduce numbers to 300 from the current 400*

(The strength of the College at present (1931) is 400 as recorded the commission Christians: 36, Non Christians: 364, total 400 Staff: European 9, Indian Christian 11, Non Christians 22 Total 42 About 180 of these were staying in five College hostels.)

The recommendations made by this high powered commission influenced many changes College has undergone in later years.

The College Buildings

The College is housed at present in one of the most beautiful buildings any institution can be proud off. The present building was built and inaugurated on 9th of January 1914 by the then Viceroy of India Lord Hardinge. Thus it is significant that it will be completing hundred years of it existence this year (2014) in January.

Chapter 2

Canon William Edward Sladen Holland: Principal 1929-1933

Canon Holland came to St. John's College with a wealth of experience from many Christian Institutions in India. He arrived at Allahabad in 1899 and established Oxford and Cambridge Hostel (Holland Hall), he served as Principal of St. Paul's College, Calcutta and thereafter Principal of C. M. S. College, Kottayam and Union Christian College, Alwaye, before joining as Principal of St. John's, Agra. He had a wealth of experience in Christian Higher education at Allahabad, Calcutta and Travencore (now part of Kerala) and had a key role in the formulation of the resolutions passed by the Agra conference of Christian educationists in 1929 which formed the basis of the formation of Lindsay Commission.

It was not an easy job for Canon Holland to succeed a towering personality like Dr. A. W. Davies who was Principal for fifteen years from 1913 to 1928 and also first Vice-Chancellor of the newly formed Agra University. He managed affairs of the College well with able support and assistance from Canon T. D. Sully as Vice-Principal. Administrative changes suggested by the Lindsay Commission were gradually being implemented during this period after careful study of its suitability for St. John's College.

The College at this stage had strength of 400 students, 212 in Intermediate classes, 129 in Degree classes and 59 in Postgraduate classes. Out of these 254 students were Hindus, 104 Moslems, 36 Indian Christians, 6 European and Anglo-Indian. About 180 of these students were living in five College Hostels and others in homes of recognised guardians. As the numbers of women students were increasing a proposal for their accommodation in a special hostel and establishment of the Queen Victoria High School for girls was under consideration at this stage and was awaiting approval of the Government.

The staff strength too had considerably increased to 42. The idea of a separate Hostel for women in the form of Davies House came into fore during his period. As a result of his experience gained in working in various parts of India he put emphasis on improving the corporate life of the Hostels in promoting and integrating students from different geographical regions to live and study together.

Canon T. D Sully: Principal 1933-1948, 1954-1955

Canon Thomas Donald Sully, nicknamed lovingly 'Papa Sully' by St. Johnians of the period and later generations venerated as 'Saint Sully', arrived in Agra towards the fag end of 1912 and joined the staff in the year 1913. He served the College in many capacities for long years before taking over its reign as its Principal from Canon Holland in the year 1933. A very humble and saintly person, he guided astutely the destiny of the College for the next 15 years, one of the most difficult periods in the world history, and particularly Indian History. Through his mild and humble yet firm manners he very successfully guided the institution through the Second World War and also during the Independence movement leading India to its freedom from the colonial British rule in 1947. His very act of stepping aside voluntarily from the Principal's position to Vice-Principal's position and handing over the reins of the College to the then Vice Principal Dr. C. V. Mahajan, an Indian who became the first Indian Principal of the College in 1947, speaks immensely of his character. He continued for a while to assist the College in the period of transition and then again stepped in as Principal for another term, 1954 to 1955 when Dr. Mahajan resigned to take over as the fulltime paid Vice-Chancellor of Agra University. He handed over the Principal's charge to Mr. P. T. Chandi in the year 1955.

Canon Sully continued to be associated with the College as member of it's Governing Body and provided inputs and advice for another decade while he remained as the Secretary of the Lucknow Diocese at Allahabad.

Youth and Leadership Training

The period of Canon Sully was a testing period that trained generations of youth in value based academics who shouldered the responsibilities of free India commendably in later years. The College Parliament and Union Society were very active and provided the much needed training to students in leadership and administrative practices. Mark Memorial Institute was established to provide much needed primary health and hygiene advice to the 'mohallas' around the College. This also gave the much needed exposure to the students about the primary health and needs of the under privileged Agraites. College also took keen interest in the activities of the International Student Services. Village camps were regularly organised in Villages like Barhan, Bhalokhara, Saiyan and the Economics department of the College under the leadership of Mr.H.L.Puxley carried out studies in rural economics. College Rural Service Union Camp at Barara, Rover Scout Camp at Almora, SCM camps at Satal are some of the activities needs special mention.

Rural Development and Establishment of Gram Sudhar Sabhas

The rural development activities started earnestly in 1933 under the leadership of Mr. H. L. Puxley. A landmark event was the introduction of Napier grass or elephant grass in the area through Agricultural Institute at Naini, Allahabad which helped in the stabilisation of the soil and preventing erosion. Initiative was also taken in introduction of improved varieties of seeds for other crops. Extensive studies were carried out in twelve selected villages in changing pattern of tenancy, agricultural indebtedness, storing grains, canals and irrigation facilities. The results were published in the form of a book 'Agricultural Marketing in Agra District' by Longmans Green & Company a publication which became very handy for even government officials in early development activities in the area.

Rural Development became a thrust area for the College with the leadership of Economics Department especially under Mr. H. L. Puxley and Prof. R. S. Dwivedy. Twelve Villages with Village Sahta as the central village and adjacent villages of Thapi, Kathwari, Atus, Khandwi, Nagar, Sahai, Rasulpur, Pali, Sakatpur, Nanpur, and Anguti were selected for the work. College provided three teachers of the economics department who camped in the villages for a three month period in a year supervising batches of students from the college in village work, cleaning village streets, organising games for village students and also showing lantern slides to educate them. Villagers were organised in to Gram Sudhar Sabhas. Hygienic conditions in these villages improved as a result of Soak pits made mostly by the 'shramdan' by volunteers from the college and the villagers. The Gram Sudhar Sabhas gained semi leagal status in many villages and their authority and decisions were accepted in minor dispute resolution in villages. They played a positive role in village administration.

'One of the remarkable achievements of the college work in the Circle was the initiation and completion of holdings in Villages Sahta and Thapi in 1937. This was achieved aganist serious obstacles thrown by Patwari and Zamindar's agent aganist the measure' (Dwivedi-Rural Development Work-1967).

Inter-village sports were organised by the College students in 1936 in which the village and the population actively participated. The competitions were held in races, jumps, tug-of-war, kushti (wrestling) and the then Commissioner of Agra Mr. Dible distributed prizes. The spirit created through these activities helped in creating a positive comradarie in the entire region which helped in the development work.

Social Service League

The College Social Service League was started in 1924 by Prof. Herbert Mark the then Vice-principal of the College for developing sensitiveness in students and also up-lifting of the poor and not so rich in the urban and rural surroundings of Agra. This humble beginning gained momentum with the establishment of the Mark Memorial Hut in honour of Prof. Mark (after the untimely demise of Prof. Mark) on a piece of land acquired by the College on the road to Belanganj. A small dispensary was established there and Students on a regular basis visited urban bastis and provided primary medical aid. The volunteers worked for improving the living conditions of the underprivileged making Mark Memorial Hut as a base. Primary Health Aid was provided to the needy by student and staff volunteers on a regular basis. The Social Service League gained status and admiration from the public and served as training and sensitising ground to the students in social work. The students union set apart 20% of its income and the staff and the students voluntarily contributed liberally to meet the expenses of the centre.

The Municipality of Agra too recognised the work and used to make budget allocation for this work. The present day NSS has derived its strength and structure mostly from the Social Service League and the government of UP as well as at Delhi used the experiences of the Social Service League of the College when the NSS programme was put in place officially at a later stage in the sixties and seventies.

Some happenings of the period are worth mention.

In 1939 floods overwhelmed Agra. Out- lying areas of the city and even parts of the City was inundated by the floods. The College buildings became shelter for over 400 families, teaching was suspended and the College family got fully engaged in flood relief work for more than three weeks. The College was blessed also by the visits of Canon

A.W. Davies, former Principal and founder Vice Chancellor of Agra University. Bishop W. J. Thomson, serving as Bishop of Iran who also was an engineer by profession and had a major role in the building of the main College building during 1910-1914 also visited the College.

The second world war was at its peak and resulted in the call of H. L. Puxley of the economics department for war services in 1941. The College continued with activities like participating in the UTC camp at Allahabad, Rover Scout Camp at Almora, and Rural Service Union Camp at Barara. Two staff members who joined the staff in 1941 were Prof G. L. Mukerji of the History Department and Miss M. A. Bald of English Department, both had long years of distinguished service at the College later.

1942 was a year with unusual happenings in the College. Political storm was brewing in Agra and the College has to be closed in August for a few days as a result. Confusion prevailed for a while which was overcome by better counselling and normal functioning started in September. College also mourned the death of Harry Davies son of Canon A. W. Davies former Principal while serving as an officer on Destroyer Electra sunk in the battle of Java by the Japanese.

The Union Society and its role in training and moulding the future leadership was immense and could be better understood in the words of the president of the Society in 1938-39 in his farewell address. "The duties of a President of an institution like our Union Society are rather heavy because he has to combine many heterogeneous and fissiparous elements and act both as a judicial and executive head. The training that we get, however, is more precious than the actual work we have to do. The foremost idea that loomed before me when I began work was how to pluck popularity out of honesty and I can very frankly admit that I discovered it be an achievement beyond the reach of a man of my caliber..."(Mohd Yunus Naqui V Eng). Testing students caliber in leadership was the main objective of the Society from the early formative years and the institution and the staff tried to achieve this earnestly.

To understand the real driving spirit of the College during this period we reproduce in part the Address given by Canon Sully at the Farewel to Examinees-1949 (College magazine 1949-50)

"Looking back over two or more years of College life, or looking forward into the rather doubtful and uncertain future, I wonder what are the things which are or should be uppermost in our minds at this farewell gathering today. As this is the last occasion on which I shall share such a meeting as a member of the College myself, I am going to give my own answer. It would start from some of those characteristics which belong to a comparatively small College such as we have tried to be, though it has not been easy to restrict our number to what in earlier days would have been considered to be the limit for a small college. Yet even as it is with 700 hundred or more on our enrolment, there are certain features of our life which you may have noticed, and which become much more noticeable by contrast with the life in the over- crowded Colleges and Halls elsewhere.

There are values in education, well known and treasured in the ancient systems of this land which are liable to be neglected, or even lost, in the modern developments of this age. I would mention three characteristics in particular:-

(a) There are more friendly contacts between students within a relatively small student community with its social, intellectual and athletic activities, its membership of hostels, teams and committees. Such contacts extend across many divisions of faculty, class and sex, of community and even of race. Much of our most valuable learning is not of books but of men and within the limits of student life you have learned in this way something of the many –sided life and culture of your country. You may have learned to understand and appreciate those who differ from you. I remember how in the very year when our hearts were saddened by the bitter strife between the communities, the three- legged race in hostel sports in one of our College hostels was won by a Hindu and a Moslem student with legs tied together and arms locked, not in strife but in friendly cooperation.

(b) Similarly amid smaller numbers there can be that more personal contact and relationship between teachers and students, which has been a treasure in the ancient tradition of India. Difficult enough, no doubt, under the modern pressure of numbers and finance, and additional work which so many teachers have to undertake if they are to make both ends meet. But it becomes practically impossible under the conditions of mass –teaching which obtain in some of our larger centers. Here you still have the opportunity to know your teachers and your teachers to know you, and there may be a sharing of values both of personality and learning, and not merely utilities of lecture notes and cram books.

(c) There is, thirdly, the more organised life of the small college, in which most if not all can have a share; for the organisation is itself personal rather than mechanical. A college society begins and develops under the personal stimulus of an individual student or teacher, a small group of keen men; and its activities carry that special value which arises from the sharing of the best things in learning and life.

'It was a most significant 'experiment with truth' which Gandhi-ji first made in South Africa at Phoenix and Tolstoy Farm, when he gathered a group together to be his close companions in a common life, and then to form as a close –knit body an effective instrument of 'satyagraha': It was far more difficult to accomplish on the vast scale of the national movement in this country, but he continued to employ the method so far as he could. And it was to insufficient corporate preparation of this kind that he was wont to attribute those failures which with characteristic humility he spoke as 'Himalayan Blunders'. There is a real danger today that in a too rapid and ill-prepared expansion of education we may find further blunders of a Himalayan dimension perpetrated,- blunders not easy to correct and remedy.'

Similarly he saw the danger of an over-mechanized industrial system and in our growing reliance on machinery for everything. In contrast the relatively simple and independent life of the old Indian village community always had its attractions for him, as containing values of at all costs to be conserved; and the simple 'takli' and spinning wheel became a symbol of a productiveness which had not lost its individual and personal character. We should follow with intense interest the modern experiment of a 'Panchayati Raj', and some of you may have opportunities of helping that to be a real achievement and not one of the many paper schemes which seem to get us so little further.'

Canon Sully further said 'we have to face frankly all those factors which stand in the way of the cultivation of community and friendly relations, whether between individuals or classes or nations. The world, and our country in particular, is full of broken fellowship, were hatred has become entrenched and it is hard indeed for the individual to escape the intense communal influences which make for strife. Some of these more ancient divisions have hardened into walls of caste and race, gathering about them whole masses of associations of superiority and inferiority, of cleanliness and uncleanness.

We see that the leaders of the period made a conscious effort to lead the College family, in a very sensitive way, keeping in mind the politico-social changes that are taking in place all around and also the need for producing quality leadership for an emerging free nation.

We should realise that these words spoken by Canon Sully in his farewell address after long association with St. John's College for decades, in various positions more than 50 years, have proved to be prophetic and very much relevant to contemporary India and is also the philosophy behind the very existence of the St. John's College. Canon Sully's continued association in one way or other provided the much needed stability when changes were taking place all around especially in the political atmosphere.

Chapter 3

Mr. C. V. MAHAJAN, M.A (Oxon), - First Indian Principal: 1948-1954.

Prof. C.V. Mahajan took over as Principal soon after India became independent. He was also the Second Principal of the College who later became the Vice Chancellor of the Agra University and also elected as a member of the legislative council of U.P.

Dr. Mahajan was a strict disciplinarian and administered the College with firmness. He was ably supported by a dedicated band of staff whose contribution to St. John's reaching greater heights is difficult to assess. There was a determined effort by the staff of the period (to name a few: Prof. S. P. Sharma, Mr. J. B. Dorab, Mr. H. H. Tandon, Mr. H. H. Quadri, Prof. J. C. Talukdar, Prof. C.T. Gideon, Shri. A. P. Misra, Prof. C. R. Chaturvedi, Prof.P. T. Chandi, Canon T. D. Sully, Mr.S. C. Chaterji, Miss M. E. Gibbs, Mr. H. S. Houseman, Prof. R. S. Dwivedi, Rev. N. Thimothy, Dr.J. Chandra, Mr. K. N. Bakaya, Mr. M. U. Faridi, Dr. L. P. Mathur, Prof. N.M. Mukerji, Dr. M. S. Mani, Prof. N.M. Anthani, Mr. A. R. Tiwari, Dr. P.I.Itteyerah, Prof. M. A. Hakim, Mr. B.V. Paul, Mr. K. John Kurian, Prof. Ambika Charan Sharma, Mr. S. K. Singh, Dr. V. P. George) to raise the standards of teaching, research and related activities associated with learning to higher levels.

Prof Mahajan was elected as Vice-Chancellor of the Agra University in November 1949. The esteem at which Prof. Mahajan was held by all at that time is reflected in the Address presented to him by the St. John's College Union on the 19th November, 1949. I reproduce here part of it as 'Sir,

We are proud of you, Sir, proud of our College and therefore proud of ourselves at this singular honor College has achieved in contributing a Second Vice- Chancellor to the University from among our worthy principals. In felicitating you, Sir, we are felicitating ourselves for between you and us, the bonds of affection, confidence and understanding are so intimate that in achieving this distinctive honor, we feel honored ourselves.

You will pardon us, Sir, for taking this opportunity and using our liberty to express our sincere feelings towards you. You are, Sir, well known for your stern sense of descipline which makes our College a premier institution in the University, so far as this quality is concerned; but let us assure you Sir, this is not at the cost of sympathy and understanding which like a magnet draws us closer to you. It is an undisputed fact that the freshers have no hesitation in approaching you, confident of considerate and paternal treatment.

As a teacher, you have been an ideal mentor drawing us out of ourselves and creating a new interest in our studies, but this election of yours, will we are afraid, leave you less time to devote to the task by natural inclination and aptitude you have been pre-eminently, by nature endowed. Your dignity, seriousness, sense of duty and love of truth and justice has become a pattern on which we would do well to mould ourselves,

Your devoted and obedient students of St. John's College

Mr. Mahajan was a true educator. The Haileybury lecture delivered by him in 1939 as a member of the staff is a proof of this. About the Union Society he asked the students:

"consider the Union Society. Have you given much thought to the purpose for which the Society exists. It is not just a joke, but have an educative value. It gives you some training in organising yourselves, managing your own affairs, making a right choice of those whom you wish to hold office, public speaking and conduct of meeting. In other words, the union society meant to give you some training in the performance of those civic duties which you will be called upon to do when you pass out into the wider world." Valuable lessons are taught for democratic institution to work. You cannot be made democratic by law. He concluded reminding the audience of the lines of Rudiyard Kipling

"Land of our Birth, we pledge to thee,
Our love and toil in years to be;
When we are grown and take our place
As men and women with our race
Father in Heaven who lovest all,
Oh help thy children when they call;
That they may build, from age to age,
An undefiled heritage."

Natural History Society was established in with 1949 with the encouragement and support of Dr. Mahajan and became very active in subsequent years.

Establishment of School of Entomology in 1950 which gained international acclaim in later years is a land mark event that had happened with active support of Dr. Mahajan in 1950.

Canon Dr. P. T. Chandi: Principal 1955-1968

The outstanding Principal of St. John's College during the post independent period is un- doubtably (Padma-shree) Rev. Dr. Panavelil Thomas Chandi. Rev. Chandi took over the Principal-ship with a treasure of experience and ample training in leadership with tenures at St. John's College, Agra as Games Superintendent, Bursar and Vice Principal, at Foremen Christian College, Lahore as Prof. of Mathematics and St. Andrews College, Gorakhpur as its Principal. He gained experience and matured as an able administrator by working in different positions in colleges he served and understood the student psychology and management by working intimately with them specially as Warden and

**Principal Chandi with Prime Minister
Nehru at the opening of the new Block**

Superintendent of Games where contact with students were maximum. He also had the privilege of interacting and working with many educationists and community leaders by associating with their managements.

The Builder: Centenary Wing, College Central Library, Steele Kothi Compound Staff Residences, Post Graduate Wings of Zoology and Chemistry and the new Library block are structures came up during his period.

Principal Chandi took over as Principal in 1955 from Canon Sully in 1955 who had taken over the Principalship for a year as a stop gap arrangement when Prof. C.V. Mahajan left the position to take up higher responsibilities as Vice Chancellor of Agra University and later also as member of the Union Public

Priminister Nehru opening the new block

Service Commission subsequently. The period under Rev. Chandi's leadership saw the College climbing new heights and was graded by the UGC as one among the best ten colleges in the country(Dr. C. D. Deshmukh-Chairman UGC). The College also could complete its symmetry by building the office block (Centenary block) a dream left incomplete by Canon Davies, the builder of the present building. He also took up the challenge of constructing an independent Library building, a new beautiful College Chapel and also added new buildings to science

The foundation stone of the college centenary wing was laid by
Dr. S. Radhakrishnan then Vice-President of India.

departments for their post-graduate expansion. He
considered providing accommodation to the staff in the
campus as a priority and new staff residences were added
in the Steele Kothi compound. It enabled the Institution to
attract better senior staff in residence to strengthen teaching
and research. The ratio of residential students also increased
making the college a mini India with students from all parts
of the country staying in five hostels including Davies House
exclusively for women students.

Distinguished Visitors

A stream of distinguished visitors visited the College
during this period and addressed the students including
Dr.Sarvapilli Radakrishnan as then Vice-President of the
country, who laid the foundation stone of the Centenary
wing, Pt. Jawaharlal Nehru our first Prime Minister who
inaugurated the wing, Mrs. Vijaylaksmi Pandit, the first
women president of the United Nations, to inaugurate the
new Library Building and also opened the Science

Principal Chandi with Mrs. Gandhi

Principal Chandi with Chester Bowles

Exhibition. The College convocations were addressed by stream of distinguished personalities like Arnold Toyanbe, historian, Rt. Rev.Arthur Michael Ramsay, Arch Bishop of Canterbury, Dr. M. C. Chagla, Union Minister of Education, Dr. C. D. Deshmukh, Chairman of UGC, Dr. M. S. Kothari, Chairman of UGC, Governors of Uttar Pradesh at the given period, Mr. Chestor Bowls, and Paul

Galbrieth distinguished ambassadors of United States of America, Dr. Zakir Hussian, Shri. V.V.Giri, both former Presidents of India, Mrs. Indira Gandhi, former Prime Minister of India, Shri Morarji Desai, former Deputy Prime Minister of India, International Scientists J. B. S. Haldane and Theodosius Dobzhansky also visited the College during this period.

Sir Arnold Toynbee, the eminent Historian, delivering the convocation address—Feb. 1957.

The wisdom shared by the distinguished visitors not only enriched the students but the functions organised for their visits were training grounds in organisation for a stream of student volunteers and staff members of the period alike.

Seminars and Lectures (stress on academic excellence)

Principal Chandi stressed and strived to mould generations of students and staff under his care to have questioning minds without becoming physically 'question marks' (?) themselves as he used to say. He organised special postgraduate assemblies twice a week for those who are not covered under compulsory daily general Assemblies due to space limitation in the assembly hall. These assemblies were often used to be addressed by invited educationists and followed by open discussions. He also carefully, through various departments, chose students with ideas and ability to address these assemblies there by training and sharpening the minds of students.

Canon Davies last visit to St. John's College

Research Activities

This period show a thrust in research activities mainly due to the encouragement given by the management specially the Principal. Funds were made available to Departments and were encouraged to take up various research projects which resulted in creation of a very positive atmosphere in the College. Staff Members and students were given utmost support and encouragement to take up research which resulted in national level activities.

Research Students and Staff members involved in research work in various departments were required to organise and address inter-departmental seminars on their topics of research so that other departments of the College too got an opportunity to know about the work they are involved in. Questions could be raised by any one from the audience including staff members of other departments and others invited for the seminar. Postgraduate departments looked forward to these Friday seminars that were often attended by Dr. Chandi himself sitting in the audience. These seminars contributed immensely to raise the academic atmosphere, confidence and activities in the institution to a higher level. Formulation of a number of research projects in departments which gained funding from national and international funding agencies like the UGC, CSIR, ICAR, US-Pl 480 Projects under USAID was a result of this seeding activity initiated by Principal Chandi.

Research Projects-Pl-480 Project on Leaf-Miners, Manali Trip

I am tempted to recall here our experiences with Rev. and Mrs. Chandi on a field trip to the interiors of North-West Himalaya in Himachal Pradesh in hunt for insects as it gives an insight into the reasons for his success as Principal. Our Pl-480 field research team consisted of Dr.Ipe M.Ipe (Senior Research Officer) late Dr.S.K.Beri and Dr.Pramod Kumar Garg (Reasearch Officers) under the leadership of Dr. Santokh Singh as Principal Investigator, was on a trip for hunting leaf-miners (Agromyzidae) to northwest Himalaya. As usual we informed Principal Chandi of the proposed trip and to our surprise he expressed his wish to join us for a month old trip. We were surprised and also apprehensive of the Principal and wife being with us for such a long period in the wilderness and with only our tented accommodation at places. Our mode of transport was a Jeep with trailer containing our two tents, collection kit and kitchen utensils as we used to cook our own food. How four of us including Driver cum mechanic Aziz and Mr. Chandi and Mrs. Chandi could undertake this long road trip to from Agra to Pathankot, Dalhousie, Kalatop, Kahjhair,Chamba, Palampur, Mandi, Aut, Kulu and Manali (the present road via swarghat was not in existence then) could accommodate and undertake we were worried. But the way they adjusted in the vehicle for long and tough drive and contributed to the success of the trip is difficult to narrate. The way they adjusted to the tented life and eating sitting or the collection trunks in the kitchen tent was remarkable. They managed the whole period almost a month with two sets of clothes, washing them and using them again and again. Mrs. Chandi contributed her lot in economising the kitchen budget even checking the kitchen help Mehtab in the use of matches 'Mehtab tum beedi cum peetha hai, matches khati hai' she used to check him in her broken Hindi.

Our usual practice was to divide the total food expenses equally among the number of persons in the party and Rev. Chandi insisted on paying two shares one for himself and other for Mrs. Chandi. They adjusted to our tight schedule of field work moving from one place early in the morning to a new place and settling down by evening and then collecting specimens from there for the next two days subject to the suitability of vegetation. They joined us in our field work without any complaint travelling through horse tracks and so called jeep tracks in adverse terrain. We covered the entire area spanning from Pathankot through

Dalhosie-Kalatop- Kajhaiar-Chamba- Palampur-Sundernager-
Mandi-Aut-Kulu-Manali-Kothi-Rohtang-Pathlikul-Naggar-
Larji and Mannikaran and felt that the time is too short. The
entire trip has been very useful in collecting valuable ecological
data and new Agromyzid species hitherto undescribed above
all it helped us to understand the secret of Rev. Chandi's
success, honesty, simplicity and adjustability.

Exhibitions

Principal Chandi took a keen interest in organising
exhibitions with the total involvement of staff and students.
Science Exhibitions became a regular annual feature and
insistence of total involvement of the student community
helped in unearthing hidden talents among students. These
exhibitions were given the status of educational extension work
and also gave full credit and encouragement to the students.

Convocations and Functions:

Regular Annual College Convocations and other
functions like Terminal Evensongs, Farewell to the
Outgoing Students, Union Society Inaugural and Annual
Functions and numerous other Society Functions at various
Departments and Hostel levels, all were given importance
and opportunities of inter-action within students and also
exposure of students to outside educationists.

Each Hostel was encouraged to organise an
Inaugural Function and an Annual (Closing) Function
attended by the Principal and invited guests. This
gave the inmates an opportunity to exhibit their
talents. There existed a very healthy competition

**Prof Gideon Vice Principal, Mr. Chester Bowles,
P.D. Gupta Vice Chancellor, Principal Chandi**

between the hostels and the quality of the programmes put up by them was of very high standards. There was a scramble to get invited to these functions and often guest cards for the functions were paid by the guests them-selves!. The training in leadership and organisational skills it provided for students and the Wardens is difficult to quantify. For the College Convocations often an International or National dignitary with relevance to the field of education was invited. Organising Committees were formed well in advance with staff and students to take care of arrangements which gave a boost to the team spirit and a spirit of co-operation within the College family.

In the words of Dr. Santokh Singh a former Head of Zoology and Entomology and also an old boy of the College 'the sense of belonging to the St. John's Family was demonstrated in no uncertain terms at the time of the

College Convocation. It used to be a real treat to watch the entire Teaching staff, Secretarial and other supporting staff along with students, working together as a well oiled machine to make the function a grand success. I may be permitted to narrate an interesting remark made by a couple of students occupying the last benches in the convocation pandal. The Governor of U.P.in the course of his address said that he wondered how the College was able to maintain such an excellent discipline, the boys responded 'college mae admission le lo Sab, samajh jaogey.'!.

Sports and Games

There was full thrust given to sports and games, College annual sports was an event looked forward by everyone even non players. The competitions were held on an Inter-Hostel-Circle basis as day students too were organised into three Circles, Sikandra, City, and Taj Circles based on geographical regions of the City. Haileybury House, Bishop French Hostel, Lloyd Hostel and Old Hostel teams competed as hostel teams. Women students were divided into two teams, Davies House and Day Scholars. Individual Championship Cups and running shields for team competitions were provided. This process provided an occasion to identify talent and select college teams.

College also took lead in organising Inter College and Inter-University competitions and it provided an opportunity in improving the infra-structure for games in the College. Even North Zone Inter-University Championships in Basketball, Football, Cricket and Tennis were organised by the College.

AIACHE – All India Association of Christian Higher Education

The formation of AIACHE and role of Principal Chandi's as a founder member and first President of the All India Council for Christian Higher Education along with educationists like Fr.Mathias, Sr Briganza helped generations of youth, staff and students in leadership training. It nurtured next generation leadership to the already established institutions. For the new institutions specially the ones getting transformed into degree and post-graduate level it provided the much needed counselling. The leading institutions benefited through this process were Ahmednagar College, Ahmednager, American College and Lady Doak College, Madurai, St. Joseph's College, Thiruchirapalli, Sophia College Polytechnic Mumbai, Union Christian College, Alwaye, Madras Christian College and Womens Christian College, and Stella Maries College, Chennai and St. John's College, Agra. The support it provided in leadership training especially to the emerging young Christian Institutions was commendable.

Inter-institutional dialogues emerged among Protestant and Catholic institutions providing an opportunity for identifying talent and also a visionary outlook in the field and role of education. Ecumenism and Ecumenical activities got a boost and interaction among the institutions and individuals in institution helped in creating a positive outlook in institutions and community as a whole. The establishment of an institution like XLRI by Fr.Mathias at Ranchi and it the way it has risen as a national institution too was influenced to some extent by the atmosphere generated through this process.

The establishment of AIACHE and its activities tried to provide established Christian institutions ability to maintain their leadership role in post independent India. But in later years with the establishment of the IIT's and numerous other institutions at National level with Governmental funding even the established Christian Institutions found it difficult to stand up to the competition. Majority of them lost their vision and failed to adhere to the primary Aims and Objectives with which they were established. Even the props provided by the AIACHE could not be of any help.

The role of St. John's College and specially Principal Chandi in this process can be summarised in the words of Paul T. Lauby of the United Board of Christian Higher Education in Asia (Sailing in the Winds of Change 1996). "Principal Chandi' was one of the most distinguished Christian educators of this century. His active involvement in College and University education spanned more than six decades. He was a brilliant scholar and teacher, a principal of two Colleges, the first Christian Head of an Indian University, and a founder and the first president of the All India Association of Christian Higher Education. I can think of no one who had a clearer grasp of what Christian higher education is all about, and of its place in Asian Society. In his eloquent English, he was able to articulate all of this convincingly and movingly. For

half a century he was a revered statesman in the church and academy, and was respected as a leader of unquestioned integrity and dedication."

Government of India honoured him with the award of Padam-Shri on Republic Day 1965.

Principal Chandi was due for retirement from St. John's College on 30th June 1968, he was appointed Vice-Chancellor of Gorakhpur University during March 1968 a position he joined in March 1968.

Dr.P.I.Itteyerah : Principal
1968-1978

(Ph.D. in Chemistry, Agra University, 1942, Ph.D. in Chemistry University of Cambridge 1956, Fellow, Royal Institute of Chemistry, Fellow Chemical Society of London, Fellow Indian Chemical Society)

Dr. P. I. Itteyerah a brilliant scholar and teacher of Chemistry who was also the Vice-Principal under Principal Chandi took over the Principal-ship in 1968. A St. Johnian to the core, with all humility, he lead the Institution steadfastly where 'duty, right, and honour lead', and his leadership was with malice towards none and charity for all'. He strived for academic excellence

The National Service Scheme (NSS) was revamped and student volunteers of the College under the supervision of staff members regularly held classes for the needy students and those who are not covered under the regular structured scheme of education.Over twenty two education centres spread all over Agra and its surroundings established and run, after regular college hours, by the NSS of the College for mass education had attendance of over two thousand students at a time. These centres were run by student volunteers under the supervision of staff and the contributions of Dr. P. C. Maheshwari of the Commerce department in this effort needs to be commended.

The annual functions organised by these centres in the College Hall brought out unlimited hidden talent in youth who are not so privileged to have regular School or College education. The experience gained through this scheme helped in the structure and policy formation of the NSS programmes nation- wide later on. The officers of the Ministry of Education from Delhi regularly visited the College to assess the scheme as a pilot project. Dr. P. C. Maheshwari of the Department of Commerce along with a team of volunteers contributed immensely to this venture.

This period also saw addition and improvement of infra structure and facilities in various departments especially in the Science faculty. This period also was a period of consolidation. The Mahatma Gandhi Road which run through the campus was widened at the initiative of Late Rajive Gandhi and the college lost land and tree cover on either side of the road. With the compensation given by the Government for land acquisition an endowment was created as chaplaincy fund. Other endowments were also created to support annual or biannual lectures like the Bald Memorial Lectures under the auspicies of the English Department.

Annual Haileybury Lectures too got a boost during this period.

Dramatic Society, Other Clubs and Societies

The birth of the College Dramatic Society in 1977 was perhaps the most important event in the cultural history of the College. The Society was established at the initiative of Rev David Reid Thomas and Helen Reid Thomas of the English Department. It gave a boost to Dramatics in English and Hindi not only in the College, but also in the City of Agra and North India as a whole. Out station Teams from Delhi and Uttar Pradesh competed in the One-Act Play Festivals organised in the College Hall. National level Adjudicators helped in judging the plays and also organised workshops in dramatics to guide the budding actors. The Society was ably supported by a team of staff students and also interested people from the Agra public.

The plays staged included Shakespeare's 'Mid-Summer Nights Dream', 'Othello', "Macbeth"; 'Covenant with Death' by Margret Wood, 'Great Catherine' by Bernard Shaw, and 'Gogol's Government Inspector'. The spirit of Dramatics was in the air and I reproduce it in the words of the Secretary Ms Geeta Choudhary, 'the first of August 1977 saw members of the Dramatic Society walking resolutely towards Red Bungalow holding scripts of N.V.Gogol's Government Inspector for the first reading of the play. This was to be first of a series of practices which with the reopening of the College and successive auditions became more and more earnest with tickets and programmes printed and advertisements stuck on advantageous positions the play was successfully staged at the end of September. It was proclaimed an achievement by local and national news papers'.

The society also organised Festival of One Act Plays which attracted entries from many groups outside the state. Workshops on dramatics were organised along with these Festivals which gave exposure to the youth in dramatics in English as well as Hindi.

St. John's Ambulance Group

The revamping of the St. John's College Cultural Society is another important event that happened during this period. The functions organised by the cultural society gave a boost in the process of unearthing talents in the College. The competitions were held in an inter-hostel format and was adjudged by a distinguished external jury. These competitions also gave a quantum jump to quality of the Annual Functions of the Hostel considered as land mark events of any given year.

Vivekananda Vichar Mandal

Vivekananda Vichal Mandal is another active society of the college with pan objectives. The society has been active during this period with regular Meetings, Debates and Competitions

Dr. Itteryerah being greated by Dr. R. C. Sharma

organised for the students. It played a very significant and positive role in reconciling the underlying majority ethos of the society with that of the liberal aims and objectives of a Christian institution like St. John's College. It provided a platform for expression to a stream of thought that prevailed in the College although the years.

St. John's Ambulance Association too was very active in this period training youth in First Aid and Civil Defence. Dr.Basu Chautdhary of the S. N. Medical College remained closely associated with the activities and helped specially in training the youth in First Aid. The association was open to students from other institutions as well as interested people from the city on a voluntary basis.

Creation of designated Endowments

During this period special endowments were created for specific objectives: Bald Memorial Lecture Series, for a series of two lectures which was eventually inaugurated in 1980 with two lecture series by Dr. Brij Raj Singh also a distinguished Alumnus and Rhodes scholar of the College who was serving as Reader in English at Delhi University; Chaplaincy fund to look after the College Chapel activities and related expenses, this fund was designated specially from the compensation money received from the Government in –Lieu of the land acquired for the widening of the M.G.Road.

Post Centenary Silver Jubilee Thanksgiving Service.

The Post Centenary Silver Jubilee Service of Thanksgiving was held on the 12th of December 1976 attended by Staff Students and invited guests. Rt. Rev. Christopher Robinson, Bishop of Lucknow and Chairman of the Governing Body gave an inspiring address. His address was based on Thess.5.11-28 'encourage one another, help one another, and build one another up, just as you are already doing. He quoted St. Paul 'we beg you, to respect and honour those who are working so hard among you, and in the Lord's Fellowship are your leaders and counsellors. Esteem them very highly and give them your whole hearted affection for the work that they do for you. Be at peace among yourselves'

Mother Teresa at the College convocation

26th College Convocation 11th March 1978 and Address by Mother Teresa.

The simplicity of Mother Theresa and the advice she gave left a lasting impression on everyone present. Her address was extempore, so effective and simple, touching every heart and left many in the Pandal with tears rolling down their cheeks.

She gave simple stories from what she experienced and said 'this is what you and I must be to our people, they like you and me, have been created for greater things. They have been created for greater things. They have been created by the same loving hand of God to love and to be loved. So, here in Agra, find out where your people are. There are many people who need your tender hand, who need your understanding love. Let us not think that poor people, just because they are poor, are good for nothing. They are very great people. They are very lovable people.'

She concluded 'so today, I ask one thing from you young people,- 'Pray'. Don't face the world without prayer. Ask God to be your strength, your light, your love, to be your purity. For only pure heart can see God. Go with Him, put your hand in His hand.

For he has called you by His name, he has looked after you. He has given you parents to look after you. He has given you parents to take care of you. And you have been wanted. Today many children are not wanted. Abortion is nothing but being unwanted, and you have been wanted by your parents, so you owe your parents deep gratitude, and the best gratitude to show your parents is to be what they want you to be- child of God, a carrier of God's love and compassion, a light in the darkness of this world. And my prayer for you will be that you may understand that you are the future of our country, that it is you who will make it beautiful or ugly. I am sure that what you have received in this College is very beautiful. Make your life something beautiful for God'.

The showers of blessings poured out from the sky at the end of the address –rain, quite unusual in the month of March in Agra, perhaps marking the end of an era dominated by traditionalism in St. John's.

Dr. Satish Chandra Banwar: Principal 1978-79

Appointment of Dr. S. C. Banwar as the Principal of the College after the retirement of Dr. P. I. Itteyerah was perhaps a land-mark event. Prof. G. I. David, Professor and Head of the English Department officiated as Principal for a short period till the joining of Dr. Banwar.

Dr. Banwar, a Botanist belonged to Ranchi and was a sportsman himself was young and youthful compared to his predecessors like Canon Sully, Rev. Chandi and Dr. Itteyerah. He was also an ordained priest. He was a simple, liberal and sincere person with full of ideas and vigour to take St. John's College, steeped in old traditions evolved over a century, into totally a new youthful direction. Being a person not influenced by the existing systems and conservative atmosphere that existed, Dr. Banwar had the freedom and opportunity to shake St. John's out of the tradition bound administrative practices. He in a short period of time was able to remove the gap then existed between senior and junior staff, and staff students and non teaching staff. His fair and sincere intentions could be felt and the resistance for such a change was minimal. Some of the traditions bound senior staff too was willing to give it a try after seeing his sincerity of intent.

I would like to narrate two instances which will give an insight into the person who stayed just for only a few months in St. John's to be understood or assessed. The first incident is very personal but needs to be mentioned.

It was the very first day he came to St. John's for the interview of the Principal. We had seen a bearded youthful gentleman with a smiling face crossing from the Arts block to the Science block, perhaps to attend the interview for the selection of the Principal which was being held in the Library, and we were crossing the road from the Science to the Arts block to attend the morning assembly. We noticed the gentleman but never recognised him nor he us. The same evening we had invited Dr. T. Singh our teacher and former Head of the Department of Zoology and Entomology who was visiting Agra from Dehra-dun, for a meal. My younger son Chotu (Nikhil) got burned with boiling water earlier in the same day and we had taken him to the Doctor for medical attention. After giving the needed treatment we were back at home in Lloyd Bungalow where we used to stay. We were all sitting and chatting in the drawing room, around 9.00pm there was an un- expected knock at the door. I opened the door and found the same gentleman whom we saw while crossing the road with a smile and with an apology, introduced himself, 'I am your new Principal, I heard your son got a burn injury today, can I see him ?. We were so surprised at the simplicity and compassion shown by him. We introduced Dr. T. Singh to him and requested him also to join us for the meal; he stayed for a while, enjoyed the desert served and politely took leave. We were convinced at that very time that St. John's is in good hands.

The second incident I would like to mention happened during the Davies Cup Hockey match between Agra College and St. John's College being played at the Agra College grounds. It was customary for the Principals of both the Colleges to witness the match together. Being new to the traditions of the occasion, I, on behalf of the Games Department, briefed Dr. Banwar of the practices that existed. He requested that we go together to witness the match. I walked into his office in the afternoon before proceeding to the Agra College Hockey Ground, he jumped out of the Principals' chair with excitement and said 'let us go'. The College car used to take the Principal usually but he said no need of any car, we will walk along.

Being the hosts for the year, and expecting the visit of the new Principal of the Guest College, Agra College had made elaborate arrangements in addition to putting up the traditional Shamiana. A packed audience was already there to witness the match. The match had just started by the time we approached the grounds along the Mahatma Gandhi Road. As soon as we reached the grounds, Dr. Banwar, in excitement, climbed on to the wall in front of Fine Art Studio, (then Davico Sports), and started cheering our team- we too followed him on to the wall. The Host Principal and the reception staff were shocked to see a young bearded man accompanied by us, the staff of St. John's College, standing on the wall of the Grounds and cheering their team! It took some time to persuade him to move to the Shamiana on the opposite side where the host principal was waiting to receive him!. We won the match that year.

After his arrival in the campus and moving into the Principals' residence he asked whether he could borrow a sewing machine for a while, we sent it along in the day time. In the evening we decided to visit him and check whether the machine is useful. To our surprise he was busy stitching new curtains of the Principals Bungalow himself. !.

Principals' bungalow was an open house and at least once a week he invited the staff, young and the old with their family and their own cooked food to join him in pot-luck dinner. He was so fond of music of all kinds, Hindi and English and as young staff we looked forward for those evenings which almost lasted into mid-night.

He was the first Principal to conduct the College Assembly in Hindi, and also the first principal to open the College Hall for dance for the youth with strict supervision. The openness with which he invited, students and the staff alike, to join in was remarkable, though some senior staff, brought up in the old traditions, found it difficult to accept. He was very close to the youth. His stay in the College was too short, just eight months, but he left a lasting impression on the College as a whole. He was selected as the Pro-Vice-Chancellor of the NEHU central University at Shillong which he accepted with hesitation and after much debate.

It was really sad that we lost him as Principal and more so the fact that he fell victim to a bullet of an assassin of the underground Naga Movement almost a year later. The Naga Underground Movement was at its peak then.

Sports and Games

Sports and Games got a quantum jump during this period. The result was victory in the Agra University Hockey Championship for two consecutive years 1979-80 and 1980-1981 with more than half the team getting selected for the University team and two at the national level. The College also won the All India open Meena Kumari Cricket Tournament for Women in Lucknow. We participated in many tournaments including outstation ones like the Mumbey Basket Ball Tournament in Lucknow. Many of our students got selected at All India level and University and Inter-University levels.

Banwar Cup Matches

The love and affection he gained during his short stay in the College specially from the youth and the sporting community could be gauged by the way they came forward with a proposal to organise matches in his name- Banwar Cup Matches- between present students and old students in Cricket, Football, Hockey, Tennis and Badminton the very next year after his departure. Old students, sports enthusiasts themselves, raised funds for the prizes, awards and refreshments each day for teams and guests and also for a running trophy for the winners and other prizes for participants. Entire one week was set apart for the matches. It took the shape of a games festival lasting a week. The week concluded with a gala prize distribution function and cultural function put up by Old and Present students in the College Hall. We were all saddened when the nomenclature of the week had to be changed from Banwar Cup Matches to Banwar Memorial Matches a year later due to his sudden and un-natural demise.

St. Paul's Church College

Dr. Banwar gave bold leadership to the community and the way he lead the Action Committee to save the St. Paul's Church land when it came under Government acquisition was a witness to that. Under his leadership a silent Protest March was organised to the District Magistrate with the full support and participation of the entire Christian Community of Agra. Also delegations were sent to authorities in Agra and Lucknow, ultimately resulted in forcing the Government to withdraw the process of acquisition. The ownership of the land was reverted back to the Church for the building of the School, the St. Paul's Church School the predecessor of St. Paul's Church College and the Headquarters of the newly formed Agra Diocese.

Prof. G. M. Ram , M.A.(Howard): Principal 1979-1991

The sudden departure of Dr. Banwar as Principal and stepping in of Prof. G. M. Ram, a Physicist and Warden of Lloyd Hostel, surprised many. It was specially a disappointment for the youth and games enthusiasts. But Prof. Ram, with his policy of full support and encouragement for the existing programmes, and introduction of many new ones with the strong support of the AICHAE programmes for staff enrichment, could turn the atmosphere into a very positive one. He encouraged younger and middle level staff to go for various AICHAE programmes for staff enrichment. Batches of staff from the College joined these summer programmes and on their return to the College tried to implement them in the College. Principal gave full support to all of them. He encouraged various research programmes in departments and also tried to improve staff facilities. With his constant efforts, prodding and lobbying, at the UGC level many new research projects were undertaken by the staff, in all the three faculties, which also helped in improving the infra structure in Departments and for administration in the office.

New Buildings: Staff Accommodation and Biosciences Block.

Residential accommodation for teaching and supporting staff was a major problem faced by the College. He successfully worked out a scheme of dividing existing accommodation into smaller units to accommodate more staff in residence. With the introduction of post-graduation in Botany and Statistics there was pressure for class rooms and laboratory space in the College especially on the Science side. A mechanism of time-share and introduction of Zero Periods came into practice which was not appreciated by many staff- members. He persuaded the Science Departments to pool the finances available from the UGC building programmes under Five Year Plans for each Department for the construction of a new composite Block, the 'Biosciences Block'. A new three storey block of building was constructed in the space available between the Chemistry Block and the Biology Block thus by pooling the Plan Funds under the UGC expansion scheme. He persuaded the Management in leasing out the land behind the Staff Club and the Drew -Kothi to raise the matching grant to be provided by the Management. The foundation stone for the new building 'Biosciences Block' was laid by

Bishop W. O. Simon, Chairman of the Governing Body and inaugurated by the then Director of Higher Education U.P. Dr.S.K. Khanna, a distinguished alumnus of the Zoology Department of the College. The space thus created was shared by Botany, Statistics and Mathematics Departments.

Gol-Ghar

With the increasing number of women students on the Science side, need for more facilities for them was building up. Women staff under the leadership of Dr. Mrs. Agnes Ipe, (Department of Zoology), Dr. Mrs Geetha Singh (Department of Botany), Dr. Shobha Sharma (Physics Department) and Mrs. Namita Srivastava(Department of Statistics) and also with the support of the Science faculty approached the Principal with the problem for a solution and he gave full support for the immediate creation of a facility the 'Gol Ghar'. This facility was created with proper and sufficient toilet facilities and drinking water for women students.The women staff with the women students support also made provision for much needed snacks at the break period eliminating the need for them to move out of the Science Campus during daytime.

Science women Students got better organised and in later years, the Gol-Ghar, became a rallying point and nerve centre of various competitions and activities for women students on the Science side.

International Course In School of Entomolgy: Ecotaxonomy and Diagnostics of Agricultural Pests.

Organisation of an International Training Workshop in collaboration with the Commonwealth Institute of Entomology, London, was a landmark event in School of Entomology with the full support of Principal Ram. Under the leadership of Dr. Santokh Singh as Head of the Department and Dr. Ipe M. Ipe as Co-Ordinator this Course had a duration of six weeks and

trainees from, China, Vietnam, Papua New Guineau, Malayasia, Bangaladesh, Sri lanka, Mauritius besides India participated. A team of International level experts were provided by the Commonwealth Institute and the School of Entomology organised distinguished national level experts drawn up from various Universities and National Institutions. This event opened the door for many entomologists, staff and students from India, to get trained at the successive International Courses held at London. The infra-structure in School of Entomology got a quantum jump bringing it at par with International Institutes. Prof. Ram gave full support for the programme and also made many trips to the Ministries in Delhi with the Organisers to solve problems whenever they cropped up.

National Workshop on Himalayan Ecology at Manali 26-30 September 1989

The pioneering research work carried out by School of Entomology gained national and international appreciation. The Group Monitoring Workshop of the Department of Science and Technology New Delhi held at Shantiniketan (W.B) in 1986 chose School of Entomology to organise a national workshop for young scientists under the age of 35 in Himalayan Ecology. Full financial support was offered by the Ministry for this venture and School under the leadership of Dr. Santokh Singh as Director and Dr.

Ipe M. Ipe as Organiser conducted this workshop at the Mountaineering Institute at Manali (HP).

Young scientists, below the age of 35, from Andhra Pradesh, Bihar, Gujarat, Jammu and Kashmir, Madhya Pradesh,

Participants at Rohtang Pass

Meghalaya, Rajasthan, Tamilnadu, West Bengal and Union Territories of Delhi and Chandigargh were chosen as participants through a national selection process. The workshop organised field studies on an ecologically fragile elevated regions of North West Himalaya up to an elevation of 13260ft above MSL and exposed the participants in field methodologies on ecological studies under the supervision of experts. They were also given training in Scientific Project formulation and based on a follow-up programme recommended, Projects were invited and assessed for award by the Ministry in later years. It also re-established linkages to the UN programme, The Man and the Biosphere(MAB).

All Girls' Trek to Rohtang (Kullu Valley) HP.: 1988

An all girls trekking programme was organised under the leadership of Dr. Mrs. Jayati Chaturvedi of the Political Science and Dr. Mrs. Manju Bhayana of the Psychology Departments. Women students, eight of them, mostly from Arts Faculty were chosen for the trek and also to give them an experience in out-door tent life. The School of Entomology provided logistical support and facilities required.

Dr. M.S.Renick, M. A., Ph. D. : Principal 1991-1996

Dr. M.S.Renick of the Department of History took charge as Principal after Prof. Ram. Dr. Renick had joined the History Department of the College in 1961(?) after short term experiences at Wilson College, Bombay and Hislop College Nagpur. St. John's was not new to him as he had over twenty eight years of experience in the Department of History. He was the second staff Member from the Faculty of Arts to be chosen as Principal since independence, the first being Dr. Mahajahan as early as in 1947.

New Commerce Block

The construction of a new Commerce Block along the 'lovers lane' was a landmark event during this period. With the addition of new sections in Commerce there was acute crunch for class room space on the Arts side. Classes were being held even in the Chapel Annexe which was not liked by many staff members. After much deliberations and debate it was decided to build a new Block parallel to the railway line on the north side obliterating the historic 'lovers lane'. Opposing voices were raised by many old students who had emotional attachment to the pathway. Questions were also raised at our ability in creating a building matching in architecture, quality and style to the existing building of the Arts Block.

The new block proposed came up in the space where the stage for the annual convocations used to be held and also part of the then existed basket ball court. The era of annual convocations had come to an end by then due to the inability of the University to conduct and publish examination results in time. The pressure for the class room space was increasing due to the increasing number of new admissions and starting of new sections in Commerce. The situation then existed logically favoured the construction of the new block. Thus the new block 'The New Commerce Block' came into existence.

Dr. Renick had the quality of seeking and taking advice from all quarters in administering the College and facing the challenges higher education as a whole was facing during this period. We were witnessing vast changes in the pattern of education especially in higher education. Pure academic courses were no more attractive to the students, especially at the post-graduate level, as the course contents were not matching their needs. New courses in Administration, Management, Information Technology and the like, were providing them job opportunities. This resulted in the fall of attendance in the regular classes at under-graduate as well as post-graduate levels. The class room teaching was becoming redundant as students were being attracted to coaching classes and this also affected the morale of quite a few sincere teachers. The decline of the Morning Assembly, a cherished tradition by generations of staff and students also suffered as a result.

Visit of Dr.Kurshid Alam Khan

The visit of the College by Dr. Khurshid Alam Khan a very distinguished alumnus of the College 1938-42 vice patron of Delhi alumini and the then Governor of Karnataka rekindled the memories of the days of the convocation. He addressed the outgoing students in the Farewell to Examinees Function in the College Hall on 30th of March, 1993. He narrated stories of his own days in the College (he was the College Hockey Captain and also University Colour holder-1938-39) also reassured us all in his own words 'the present state of the society is not beyond redemption. This situation is our basic reason for faith and hope in the future. We have full faith in our people that they will rise to the occasion and will have the privilege to contribute their share in the enchanting task of nation building activities'.

Dr. Ipe M. Ipe, M.Sc., Ph.D., F.R.E.S., F.E.S.I: Principal- 1996- 1999

Dr. Ipe M. Ipe was an alumnus of the College from the year 1956-57 session in B.Sc. biology and had his post-graduation in 1961 in Zoology and Entomology. He continued in the Department with his doctoral work and post-doctoral work in Entomology with Scholarships and Fellowships from the Ministry of Education. He was appointed as Senior Research Officer under the first Pl-480 Scheme under the supervision of Dr. Santokh Singh. At the successful culmination of the project he joined the Department of Zoology and Entomology as lecturer and continued in the teaching faculty till his appointment as

Principal in 1996. He was the second alumnus of the College to be appointed as Principal, the first being Dr.Itteyerah.

He was well versed in traditions and practices of the College due to his experience gained as Warden, Dean of the Hostels, and Games Superintendent. His long stint as a Warden of Lloyd hostel and association with sports and games since his student days and thereafter as the Games Superintendent of the College helped him in administrative matters. Special efforts were made to bring the standards back to the levels existed previously with partial success as there was a gradual decline in the levels of late.

There was a determined effort during this period to get more involvement of staff in running the College. An increased role and participation of various Committees in Departments and the Academic Council and Staff Council in policy making was successfully attempted.

Campus improvement and improving the working ambience was attempted with some degree of success. The layout of quadrangles on Haileybury House and Bishop French Hostel were given a face- lift and redone with the active participation of staff and students. The walkways and pathways were re-laid by staff and students through 'shramdan' and especially students of the NSS of the College played a significant role in the activity. New lawns and gardens were laid and also tree plantation was made in a big scale by the staff and students to make the campus look better. A scheme for beautification of the stretch of MG road from Hariparbat to St.John's Crossing was drawn up and given to be District Administration for permission for implementation.

Student Exchange Programme

CUAC: Colleges and Universities of Anglican Communion, an International Organisation under the patron-ship of Arch Bishop of Canterbury has come into existence in the year of 1995 with objectives of increasing inter action among institutions at international level. The primary objective of this organisation was to provide opportunities for staff and student exchanges. Scholarships for Staff to study abroad, was in existence in some form like the Dansforth Scholarships and a few members of St. John's Staff were beneficiary of this in the past, but not as exchanges which was intended to be a two way process.

Student exchanges were finding roadblocks as academic programmes considerably differed in different countries. In spite of all this St. John's managed successfully to host the first exchange student Mr. James Madder from Huron College, Canada, an institution with over 130 years of standing and striving to provide university education of the highest North American standards. Mr. Madder joined St. John' for a year for an undergraduate programme with our undergraduate courses getting acceptance in the system existed in Canada with slight modifications and Huron College, Western Ontario awarding the Honours Degree with courses completed and evaluated in St. John's. A MOU was signed by the two institutions and Dr. Gyaneshwar Chaturvedi, Head of the Political Science Department volunteered the monitoring and supervision of the work of the student.

It may be of significance here to record that the subjects chosen and the syllabi formulated for the student were

Biology (Ecology and Environment), Political Science and History, far superior to that existed then in Agra University syllabus. It has been agreed to evaluate the performance of the exchange student and pass on the results to the parent University for the award of the credit. Our own Vice chancellor expressed keen interest and agreed to place the syllabus before the Academic bodies so as to facilitate students of St. John's undergoing a course in Canada and Agra University providing acceptance. In exchange one student of St. John's was to be accommodated there in Canada the same year. It was sad that our University Sessions were running far behind schedule and hence we could not complete the choice of our candidate in time!.

U. P. Government Merit Grant. After a gap of many years, College was awarded the Merit Grant of Rs. 50,000 by the U. P. Government in 1997 for good overall performance in the state.

Chapter 4

The Chapel of Invitation: A True Nursery in Ecumenism

The Chapel of Invitation originally was a Crypt Chapel below the present Chapel and was a place of true ecumenism. It provided opportunity for generations of students since 1914 to pray, worship and interact. The day in the College started with the morning worship in the Chapel always lead by a Christian member of the staff and the readings and at times intercessions shared by students. A rota for the worship with leaders and readers were prepared in advance, often for a month if not for the term and put up on the Chapel notice board and also circulated to the hostel notice boards to enable the participants to be prepared or make alternates if not available on a particular day. Principal was invariably present every day to worship along with the rest.

Old Underground Chapel

The narrow winding stairs at the back of the building lead into an underground chapel with a beautiful altar. An organ was on one side to aid in the singing. The suitable hymns corresponding to the reading for a week was selected in advance and singing practices used to be held on Saturday evenings at Paul Jackson's residence at the Haileybury House always ending with a cup of coffee and thereafter cleaning up the place. Resident students of all the Hostels enjoyed the evening and looked forwarded for the Saturdays.

The underground chapel could hardly accommodate about 60 people but the ambience inside was spiritual and electric. There was absolutely no room for disturbance of any kind and was ideally suited for quiet meditation. One of the towers on the first floor roof had a bell that could be rung with expertise from the chapel with a wire rope connection. Often student volunteers used to ring the bell in the morning while the peon delegated with the duty was late or on leave. The service used to start at 6.30 am in summer and 7.00 am in winter. The routine provided by the chapel service in the morning brought in a sort of discipline to the whole day and generations of students, especially residents immensely benefited.

The Chapel of Invitation also provided a place of worship for ethnic denominations like the Mar Thomites and Jacobites and even other splinter groups mostly from south India especially Kerala during Sundays. Once a month a visiting priest used to visit and conduct services in Malayalam. The service formats and the Hymns used to be handwritten and carbon copies used to be made according to the need. The denominations, Syrian Orthodox, Catholics and Mar Thomites all worshiped together forgetting the liturgical differences that separated them at their home churches. Arch- Bishop Athiade of the Roman Catholic Diocese of Agra Church too occasionally visited and addressed the worshipers. Holy Communion was conducted once a week on Thursdays and all worshipers took part irrespective of their parent denomination. What a wonderful experience and opportunity of true ecumenism!.

The New Chapel

In Canon Davies own words

"The College itself is widely recognised as one of the most beautiful and impressive educational buildings in India. No lower standards can possibly be accepted for the Chapel. It will probably be possible to build it by stages'". This thought expressed as far back in 1924 got fulfilled by the untiring efforts of Principal P.T. Chandi.

With the completion of the new Library building on the Science side and its inauguration by Mrs. Vijay Laxmi Pandit, the library was shifted and the space thus available was converted into the modern chapel with an additional room available for meetings and workshops and a library. The Altar which was in the underground chapel was shifted, as it is, without any damage and installed in the new Chapel thus providing continuity of worship and fellowship as had originally planned at the time of the construction of the building in 1914.

The Nativity Tableau

The annual Nativity Tableau at Christmas time put up by the collective effort of the Christian Staff and the students in the College Hall each year is an event keenly looked forward by every one. The members for the Christmas Choir was selected well in advance, the carols and hymns chosen and regular practice singing always started more than a month in advance. The characters for the tableau were mostly from the staff and students were drawn in only when the staff fell short. Regular practices were held at least for a week with readings. Full dress rehersals were held with lights and costumes and the tableau was put up in the College Hall for two days.

Wiseman Presenting Offerings

Choir

The first day it was for students and the second day open to an invited audience. This annual feature was looked forward by the entire community.

Role in Leadership Training

The role of The Chapel of Invitation in molding the Christian leadership in the country is immense. It has helped in providing numerous Church leaders, Community leaders and Institutional leaders. To mention a few, Bishop A. V. Joanathan (student of 1938)- first Bishop of Agra Diocese, Bishop John Sadiq- Bishop of Nagpur, Bishop Pritam Santram- Bishop of Delhi, Bishop Mall -Bishop of Punjab and later Moderator of Church of North India, Prof. M.O.Varkey, Principal of St.Andrew's College, Gorakhpur, Dr. John Hala, Principal of St.Stephen's College, Delhi, Dr. P. I. Itteyerah and Dr. Ipe M. Ipe-Principals of St. John's College, Agra, Prof. P. E. Deen-Principal, Christchurch College, Kanpur, Dr. A. M. Chacko -Principal of Union Christian College, Alwaye, P.T Thomas Principal Marthoma Training College Tiruvilla, Prof. E. J. John- Principal, Mar Basellius College, Kottayam, Prof. C.T. Titus- Principal, Mar-Thoma College, Thiruvalla, O A Cherian, Principal St. Thomas College Kozhencherry, Dr. T.A. George, Principal Catholicate College, Pathananmthitta, Prof. Titus Varkey- Principal, K. G. College, Pampady, and Dr.Babu Joseph- Principal, St. Thomas College, Ranni.

The Chapel life and its fellowship was enriched by quite a few others some as Chaplains and others as laymen. To mention a few: Prof. C.T.Gideon (Vice-Principal & Officiating Principal),Dr. A.R.Tiwari, Rev. Dr. K. J. Kurian (Chaplain), Miss M. E. Gibbs, Miss Brenda Carpenter, Mr. and Mrs. Paul Jackson, Rev. David Luck (Chaplain), Rev. Dr. T. P. Day (Chaplain), Rev. David Ried Thomas(Chaplain) and Dr.Helen Reid Thomas,Dr.Mrs. Agnes Ipe (Vice Principal &Officiating Principal) Dr. David Livingstone, Prof. P. P. Thomas, Dr.Jacob Tharu, Dr. Darshan Pitamber, Mr. Dayalchand, Dr. Joseph Kurian, Mr. Joseph Jacob, Rev. O. N. Chacko (Chaplain), Dr. B. Sundara Singh (Chaplain).

Chapter 5

Student Alone Initiatives

In a College like St. John's the process education is not just the teaching that is going on in the class rooms but a process of learning happening parallel to what is going on in the class rooms. Many of these educative processes are often initiated by the students themselves and staff members are just voluntary catalysts but they impact a larger student community than those who initiated it. We treat them here as 'Student Alone Initiatives'. It is difficult to assess their extent

Cover Page of We

of impact, but it is essential to mention some of the 'Student Alone Initiatives' which had very positive influence in the life of many of students of the period and the life in the College. These are, perhaps, minor movements evidently lasting a few years in the College but had much longer impact on the students of the period who were part of it and needs to be understood and mentioned as they too are part of the process of learning. There could be many more such initiatives than that are mentioned here and we apologise for not mentioning them due to lack of information.

'WE' was such a group of students, mostly undergraduates embracing all faculties in the late 1970's got together and organised themselves into a small group for activities chosen by themselves and sought the help of a very few willing staff members when problems arose. This was a period when most of the clubs and societies were active in the college and were catering very well to the needs of the student community, we thought, within well structured framework of the societies in activities other than class room teaching and learning. But the arrival of these groups on the scene indicated the insufficiency in the functioning of the existing arrangements as against the talents of students.

They organised cycle tours, bird studies in the campus and elsewhere, got together into discussions that mattered to them most. They organised themselves into publishing, writing, editing and printing raising funds to print what they wrote. A series of publication they brought out 'WE', stood out, and perhaps, contained contributions far superior to the College Magazine of the years. It is interesting to note that the majority of the group even after over forty years are in touch with each other and meet as often as they can.

The group organised themselves as Deb Mitra-Editor, Rakesh Bhatia-Sub Editor, Pradeep Agarwala-Secretary(1977) Rajiv Virmani (1978), Aruna Tiwari- Joint Secretary (1977), Sussamma Sachariah (1978),; Madhu Sudan Ragtah, Rajiv Virmani, Jasbir Singh, Ratna Sharma-Distributors, Manoj Gupta Advertiser, Arvind Anil Boaz-Publisher and Dr.(Mrs.) A. Ipe –Patron.(Vol.1 No.3. Feb.1977, Vol.2 No.1 Jan 1978).The annual function they organised in the College Hall was one of the best with totally new theme expressions.

Banwar Cup Matches

Dr. Banwar was the Principal of the College for less than a year but left a lasting impact on the tradition bound St. John's College. The very next year after his departure the students, mostly players, of the past years got together with the idea of organising matches between old student teams and the present years' teams. Their initiative prompted the Games Department to step in and provide the necessary support, thus started the Banwar Cup Matches which unfortunately had to become Banwar Memorial Matches due to the untimely death of Dr. Banwar as Vice-Chancellor in NEHU, Shillong a year later. Football, Hockey, Basketball, Tennis, Badminton and Cricket for both men and women were organised between the present day college teams and old students' teams. A running shield too was instituted. It took an entire week and later taken the form of a games carnival for an entire week. The funds needed for organisation, the prizes, refreshments etc was raised entirely by contributions collected and managed by the old students. The existing Old Boys Associations' activities were limited to organising a Festival Cricket Match between the Staff team and the present Cricket Team on Republic Day. Banwar Cup Matches provided the much needed opportunity for interaction between the past and present players through the organisation of these matches. Old players came up even with sponsorship for the needy present day players. It was an entirely student initiative activity which Games Department too got actively involved.

SFI Activism

We debated whether it needs to be included as a Student Alone Activity as 'SFI' term implies the political affiliations. But at a closer look it is evident that it was a student alone initiative which had a very positive impact on the life in the College. The initiative taken by a few students definitely helped in improving the College life and its functioning. College being an institution built more than a century ago was becoming deficient in infrastructure and student facilities compared to the new institutions that were coming up during post independence period.

A student group took the lead in highlighting the deficiencies which helped the College administration to take remedial action. The maximum impact the movement had was on the functioning of the College Library. Individuals, staff and students, were holding much more than the permitted number of library books for longer periods than prescribed and this movement helped the books to be returned for redistribution to the needy students. This also had a positive impact on improving the sanitary conditions in the College.

Chapter 6

Corporate Life

The corporate life in the College was rich as the ratio of residential students and day scholars was very good. Immediate post independence period the ratio was as good as 6:4 with four

List of stewards

List of stewards

hostels for boys Old Hostel, Haileybury House, Bishop French Hostel, and Lloyd Hostel and Davies House for girls could accommodate over 400 residents. The Hostels put together was a very positive influence in the general life of the College. The Hostels functioned as real nurseries in student management as each Hostel had two resident wardens who at all times provided the much needed counseling to the students. Stay in a Hostel was as good as undergoing any management course present day available to student at a considerable cost.

The life in a hostel was well organised and managed by the students themselves under the close supervision and guidance of the Wardens. A student joining for undergraduate course had a stay of minimum four years in a hostel if he or she took a postgraduate course. Each Hostel had at least two messes one non-vegetarian and two vegetarian messes run by an elected mess committee and mess managers often by rotation. The mess charges were often on a co-operative dividing system, the total expenditure being divided among the members and collected as mess charges by the wardens or mess managers. The menu in the mess was decided by the mess committee. There were two non vegetarian Common Messes, Haileybury Common Mess on the Arts side for Haileybury House and Bishop French Hostel and Lloyd Common Mess on the Science side for Lloyd Hostel and Old Hostel. Each resident got an opportunity to be holding a responsible management position in the Hostel management.

A Hostel Association was elected in the beginning of the session with a President, Secretary, Games Secretary and a Health Minister to look after the sanitation etc. The Association organised in-house competitions and often selected teams for College level competitions. Two senior residents were nominated by the wardens as Monitors to take care of daily attendance and sort out emergency problems in the absence of Wardens. One of the Wardens made it a point to be present at the attendance for which undergraduate students assembled in the Common Room. For post graduates the attendance slip was circulated through the Hostel Chow-ki-dar by the Monitors. Regular attendance register was maintained by the Monitors and counter signed by the Wardens. There was a self imposed discipline in the hostels. Any disciplinary problem was initially tackled by the Disciplinary Committee of the residents and only serious problems referred to the Wardens.

The living together and managing their own affairs provided the residents with self discipline and confidence. *The educative value of this process of living together is what our later policy makers failed to appreciate when by administrative decisions hostel life has been sacrificed without any careful study of its consequences.*

Day Students Organisation

Day students too were organised into Circles based on the geographic areas to which their residences belonged. Thus there were three Circles, Taj Circle, City Circle and Sikandra Circle. Each Circle had a staff member as warden for counseling. In later years the basis of organisation was changed into faculty base with Arts, Science and Commerce Faculties and Day students participated as organised teams in the Inter Hostel-Faculty Competitions. It played an important role in unearthing the hidden talents in students and selecting truly representative College Teams for various competitions.

The organised life in the Hostels and Faculties/Circles enriched the corporate life in the College immeasurably and it had a very positive impact in the general atmosphere and cohesiveness in the College.

Chapter 7

School of Entomology

School of Entomology:

Establishment of School of Entomology for researches in Entomology in 1950 which gained international recognition and acclaim as an advanced center for entomological research is an important event that occurred during this period. The School of Entomology was established for advanced center for researches in entomology by the singular effort of our then Professor of Zoology Dr. M.S Mani

**Dr. M. S. Mani. Founder Head
of School of Entomology**

The funds for the same was made available as grants by the Indian Council of Agricultural Research, and Ministry of Education goverment of U.P. The College Management under the leadership of Prof. C. V. Mahajan as Principal and also Rev. Sully gave full support to the venture. Successive Principals of the College gave full freedom and encouragement to the School in its activities. This farsighted visionary lead given by Dr. Mani gave India an Institution of international repute and a succession of entomologists to the country. Under the auspices of School of Entomology series of successful expeditions were under- taken to the North-West Himalaya in Kullu, Lahaul and Spiti and Ladakh area now in the states of Himachal Pradesh and Jammu and Kashmir. School executed numerous research projects on various aspects of entomology and ecology.

Enormous amount of ecological and scientific data were collected and published in reputed national and international publications. A very large number of species new to science were discovered, studied and published. This thrust in research established High Altitude Biology as a separate stream of studies internationally and School of Entomology as the cradle for High Altitude studies. The results were published by Dr. Mani in a series of books through international publishers. A much bigger contribution of this effort is the production of a stream of entomologists who gave leadership in the field. Dr. Mani himself was called to take up the leadership of Zoological Survey of India and the School provided over a dozen officers of the Joint, Assistant and Deputy Director levels to this government organisation alone. Generations of Entomologists from the School gave very effective leadership for studies in entomology in various Universities and Organisations and numerous research projects under taken generated a wealth of scientific knowledge.

Dr. Mani's Publications

Dr. Mani was not just an organiser and researcher, he had the ability to share the results of his research to a much wider public. He published a series of high quality reference books on high altitude biology and plant galls, two of the thrust area of his researches. They were published by international publishers which gained world wide acclaim. To mention a few:

Introduction to High Altitude Entomology: Methuen & Company, London, 1962

Ecology and Biogeogrphy in India: Dr. W.Junk NV Publishers, 1974

Fundamentals of High Altitude Biology; Oxford & IBH, New Delhi, 1973

Ecology and Phytogeography of High Altitude Plants of North West Himalaya Chapman and Hall, London and Oxford IBH New Delhi 1978

Ecology of High lands along with L.E.Giddings, Dr.W.Junk Publishers, The Hague, 1981

Ecology and Biogeography of High Altitude Insects: W.Junk NV The Hague, 1968

Butterflies of the Himalaya;Oxford and IBH New Delhi,1986

'Doyen of the High Altitude Entomologists in the world' in the words of Prof. Gorden Edwards Univ.of Colarado, Dr. Mani was not just a scientists bound by laboratory. He planned and lead by himself the first two expeditions to North West Himalaya 1954 and 1955 and also an expedition to the Altai Mountains after taking up the Deputy Directorship at Zoological Survey of India Calcutta.

Later Expeditions in 1956, 1961, 1978, 1985, 1986, 1992 expeditions were lead by Dr. Santokh Singh his student.

Some other high lights of the activities of the School of Entomology that needs to be recorded are the Research Projects undertaken and also National and International Workshops and Conferences organised by the School and also the publications brought out by it.

Research Projects Undertaken by School of Entomology were on thrust areas identified nationally.

Memoirs of School of Entomology Series

A series of Memoirs, Mem. Sch. Ent., were published the first one being on Agromyzidae, 'The Agromyzidae of India' by Santokh Singh and Ipe M.Ipe 1973. This was followed by a series of 13 memoirs on various groups and aspects of research carried out in the School.

The School of Entomology has been recognised as a strong center for researches on Diptera.

Dr.Ipe M.Ipe represented India in the International Congresses of Dipterology for three successive Congresses held once in four years since the Budapest Congress in 1986 and organised workshops and seminars on Agromyzidae and Nematocera.

Major groups on which publications have been made from the School are:

High Altitude Entomology	59
Agromyzidae (Diptera)	61
Chironomidae (Diptera)	21
Hymenoptera	57
Insect Development	13
Psychodidae and Phlebotomidae (Diptera)	05
Others	63

Entomologists of School of Entomology with year of Awards of Doctorates

1. Dr.Ms. Anna Philip	1949
2. Dr. S.P.Bhatnager	1950
3. Dr.S.N.Rao	1951
4. Dr.O.N.Saxena	1952
5. Dr. V.P.George	1953
6. Dr.Chandi Kurrian	1955
7. Dr.S.R.Deobhakta	1957
8. Dr.Santokh Singh	1958
9. Dr.H.H.N. Baijal	1959
10. Dr.V.M.Sinha	1960
11. Dr.G.S.Shukla	1961
12. Dr.Koshy Mathew	1961
13. Dr.G.P.Mukerji	1961
14. Dr.David Livingstone	1963

15. Dr.J.L.Nayyer   1963
16. Dr.Dr.S.K.Tandon   1963
17. Dr.C.S.Gupta   1964
18. Dr.Ipe M.Ipe   1965
19. Dr.S.K.Kulshrestha   1966
20. Dr.Neelm Sethi   1966
21. Dr.S.C.Kaushik   1967
22. Dr.R. R.Bahadur   1969
23. Dr.K.V.Lakshmi Narain   1970
24. Dr.P.T.Cherian   1970
25. Dr.Agnes Gideon   1971
26. Dr.S.K.Beri   1971
27. Dr.P.K.Garg   1971
28. Dr.J.P.Singh   1972
29. Dr.T.A.George   1975
30. Dr.M.C.Sharma   1975
31. Dr. Usha Sharma   1975
32. Dr.B.K.Kaul   1975
33. Dr.Neena Singh   1975
34. Dr.G.G.Saraswat   1976
35. Dr.T.C.Jain   1977
36. Dr.M.K.Mukerji   1977
37. Dr.A.K.Kulshrestha   1977
38. Dr.Y.K.S.Bhati   1977
39. Dr.S.K.Sharma   1978
40. Dr. O.P.Dube   1979
41. Dr. Alexander Lall   1980
42. Dr.K.V.S.Verma   1980

43. Dr.N.K. Sahani	1980
44. Dr.Gayatri Wattal	1982
45. Dr.Dhiraj Singh	1982
46. Dr.Nighat Sultana	1982
47. Dr.Anand Kumar	1983
48. Dr.Sadruddin	1984
49. Dr.Ram Kishore	1984
50. Dr.Cicy Mamen	1987
51. Dr. Girish Maheshwari	1987
52. Dr.Sreevatsa	1987
53. Dr.Sanjeev Kumar	1987
54. Dr.Gurdarshan Singh	1987
55. Dr.Johnson Varkey	1988
56. Dr.Indrapal Singh	1989
57. Dr.John George	1989
58. Dr.S.P.Singh	1990
59. Dr.Suresh Babu	1990
60. Dr.Geeta Agarwal	1990
61. Dr.P.C.Sebastian	1991
62. Dr. Dinesh Lal	1993
63. Dr.Naveen S. Singh	1993
64. Dr.Prabha Manwani	1994

High standard and momentum in researches in basic entomology, ecology and allied topics were maintained under the leadership of Dr. M.S.Mani, Dr. T. Singh, Dr. Santokh Singh, Dr. Ipe M. Ipe and Dr. Mrs. A.Ipe.

Chapter 8

Alumni

Founding Fathers and early administrators of the College realised the value and relevance of its alumni and it is evident from the fact that regular meetings of the old boys used to be held and their well being reported in the meetings. Also at the time of admissions each year special care was taken to admit students connected with the existing or old students. This in the present context and definition will appear as nepotism but helped building up a wider College family even outside the College walls. Principal's note in the College Magazine of successive years had a detailed report on the old students, their placings and well being.

The College Convocations were held regularly and along with that reunion of the old students. Principal along with staff members, many of them old students, participated. Old boys got updated with the events and happenings of the year in the College and a report on their well being and present placings were presented by the Principal. Statements of Accounts of the year used to be invariably placed before the gathering and got approved.

A treasure of information regarding old students is hidden in the College magazines but it is not possible to go into them in this volume. Publication of the College magazines became irregular in the latter part of the century.

With diminishing contents of historic value in these volumes it has not been possible to draw much details from them.

Off late functioning of the Old Boys Association has become a bit dis-organised and limited to a festival Cricket Match between the Staff Team and the Old Boys Team on the Founders Day, 16ᵗʰ of December.. Business meetings and elections are rare which is very unfortunate.

St.John's College, Agra Alumni Association, Delhi

St. John's College, Agra, Alumni Association, Delhi was formed by Old Students mostly residents of Delhi to update themselves of the well beings of members. The Association had Dr. Shankar Dayal Sharma, a distinguished Alumni and President of India as Chief patron and Shri Khursid Alam Khan, Governor of Karnataka as its Patron. The members met on a regular basis and also celebrated social occasions. Silver Jubilee of the Association was celebrated in 1999 with a get together and publication of a Souvenir and Directory of Members. The Souvenir contains reminiscences of members of their time in the College.

The Executive Committee of the Jubilee year consisted of Hon. Shankar Dayal Sharma, Former President of India, Chief Patron, Hon.Khurheed Alam Khan, Governor of Karnataka, Patron, Mr. Neepesh Talukdar, President, Mr. G.N.Gupta, Vice-President, Mr. Akhileshwar Nath, Secretary, Mr. K K Mathur, Treasurer, Mr. R.K.Khandelwal, Mr. P.P.Bagchi, Mr. Raj Narain, Ms.Tej Prabha Chandra, Mr. Pradeep Agarwal, Members and Dr.Ipe M.Ipe, Principal of St. John's College as Ex- Officio Member

President's Reception at Rashtrapati Bhawan

President Shankar Dayal Sharma, before laying down his presidency invited the members for a reception in the Rashtrapati Bhavan and majority of members participated.

St. John's College Agra Kerala Chapter-Alumni

A Southern Chapter of the Alumni has been very active with regular Annual meetings of members. An exhaustive Directory of members with their photographs and details of the stay in St. John's College was published and is a very useful publication. The annual meet was followed as far as possible by a social gathering of the families.

Inauguration of Session of Kerala Chapter

Prof. K.M.Mathew Professor of Chemistry, St. Thomas College, Kozhencherry, a 1966-68 Chemistry post-graduate took a very active role in the organisation of activities. The get together was organised in two sessions, a session with a key note address by an past distinguished alumni, sharing of information regarding members in the first session and the social part in the second post lunch session.

Chapter 9

The Essence of St. John's College

(Through Seven Decades: 1930 to 1999)

Trying to put together the story of St. John's for the seven decades from 1930 to 1999 has been a challenging job. We thought it may be helpful to understand what St. John's strived to achieve through highlighting some of the happenings and quotes by distinguished visitors during this period on special occasions and College convocations.

The first two decades of this period from, 1930 to 1950 are perhaps the most challenging period for the institution and the nation, with the freedom movement at its peak. The college visualized by many as one being administered and run by foreign missionaries steered clear of political controversies and managed to provide the much needed educated leadership post independence. We feel that the humble, honest and upright leadership provided by Canon Sully as principal from 1933 to 1948 provided the stability that required and enabled the college to come out successfully during this period. Among the students passed out from the college during this period include one past President of India, many Governors of the states, Central and State ministers, many Justices of higher courts, officers heading the Departments of State and Central governments and Armed Forces, and above all, many liberal minded community leaders belonging to all shades of belief. We have tried to put together some significant happenings, talks and addresses given by visitors- highlighting what the College was striving to achieve.

The Address delivered by Canon Sully at the Farewell function summarises greatly what St. St. John's meant for and struggled to maintain during that period. We reproduce here partially the Farewell address delivered Canon Sully after stewarding the institution for 15 long tumultuous years in the history of our country – 1933 to 1948.(College Magazine 1949 – 50 with the editor board of Mr. J.B.Dorab, Mr. H.H. Tandom and Mr. H.H. Quadri) PP 30 – 33)

"As this is the last occasion on which I shall share such a meeting as a member of the College myself, I am going to try to give my own answers. It would start from some of those characteristics which belong to a comparatively small college such as we have tried to be though it has not been easy to restrict our numbers to what in earlier days 700 or more on our enrolment, there are certain features of our life which you may have noticed, and which become much more noticeable by contrast with the life in the overcrowded College and Halls elsewhere. There are values in education, well known and treasured in the ancient systems of this land, which are liable to be neglected or even lost, in the modern developments of this age. I would mention three characteristics in particular:-

a) There are more friendly contracts between students within a relatively small student community with its social, intellectual and athletic activities, its divisions of Faculty, class of sex, of community and even of race. Much of our most valuable learning is not of books but of men and within the limits of student life you have learned in this way something of many sided life and culture of your country. You may have learned to understand and appreciate those who differ from you. I remember how in the very year when our hearts were saddened by the bitter strife between the communities, the three legged race in the hostel sports in one of the College Hostels was won by a Hindu and a Muslim student with legs tied together and arms locked, not in strife but in friendly co-operation.

b) Similarly amid smaller numbers there can be that more personal contacts and relationship between teachers and students, which has been a treasure in the3 ancient tradition of India. Difficult enough, no doubt, under the modern pressure of numbers and finance, and the additional work which so many teachers have to under-take if they have to make both ends meet. But it becomes practically impossible under the conditions of mass teaching which obtain in some of our larger centres. Here you still have the opportunity to know your teachers and your teachers to know you, and there may be a sharing of values both of personality and learning, and not merely of utilities of lecture notes and cram books.

c) There is thirdly, the more organised life of the small college in which most if not all can have a share, for the organisation itself personal rather than mechanical. A college society begins and develops under the personal stimulus of an individual student or teacher, of a small group of keen men and its activities carry that special value which arises from the sharing of the best thing in learning and life.

It is a most significant 'experiment with truth' which Gandhi ji first made in South Africa at Phoenix and Tolstoy Farm, when he gathered a group together to be the companions of a common life, and then to form a close knit body an effective instrument of Satyagraha. It was far more difficult to accomplish on a vast scale of national movement in this country, but he continued to employ the method so far as he could. And it was to insufficient corporate preparation of this kind that he went to attribute those failures with characteristic humility he spoke of 'Himalayan Blunders'. There is real danger today that in a rapid and ill prepared expansion of education we may find further blunders of Himalayan dimension perpetuated- blunder not easy to correct and remedy."

The Centenary Wing

The completion of the symmetry of the magnificent college building by the addition of the Centenary block was an event of significance having an impact of the College life and its status as having one of the most admired buildings of in the city.

The foundation stone of the wing was laid by Dr. S. Radhkrishnan, Vice-President of India on 8th of February, 1958. One of the prayers used at this ceremony sums the substance of what the college is meant for "that its foundation may be laid in truth and uprightness, that beauty and reverence may be built into its walls, and that so long as one stone remains upon another it may ever stand for all things that are pure and lovely and of good report."

Our first Prime-minister Pt. Jawaharlal Nehru inaugurated the building on 9th of October, 1959. He said "I have come here gladly on this occasion because, I am impressed as most of us must be impressed, by 100 years of constant effort and endeavor in a place of education and where this type of effort has taken place continuously over a long period of time, I imagine all kinds of thoughts gather and a place become something more than even traditions which have gathered around it. The very air of the place becomes laden with those generations of students and teachers who have come, taught each other and given place to new generations. More especially where this has been done in a true spirit of searching for the truth and with a measure of humility that place gets something like- shall I say- the aura of a place of worship, a temple".

"I have therefore come to pay tribute to this institution and to the great work it has done in the past and which I am sure it will continue to do in days to come"

The visit to the College by Archbishop of Canterbury, Most reverend Michel Ramsey and his convocation address on 4th December 1961 is another feature needs highlighting. His address on FREEDOM, BREADTH and WONDER drew spellbound attention of a very distinguished gathering. He explained these three words with simplicity and clarity.

Freedom: He said "Now, at the popular level, you are students do enjoy freedom to a degree that is quite marvellous when you consider the full course of human life. I wonder if you realise what a glorious freedom you have during your student days. Not that you have everything your quite own way for I did notice the word 'discipline' in the Principal's report at one point. Yet how greatly you do things in your own way!. You chose yourselves the subjects you are going to study. You chose very largely the way in which you are going to study them. You are free, free-free to need no books whatsoever. You are free to pick up your own companions. You join this or that political clubs or groups. You are free in quite a wonderful ways. Do realise it, because believe me when the pressures of professional life settle upon you, you won't find so much freedom of that kind. You will find that life is far less like a bicycle, wobbling this way and that way at will and far more like a tramcar where your course is determined by all sorts of events over which you have no control at all. Cherish this academic freedom which is yours. Yes; it is not as simple as that. You will find in your freedom there are certain difficulties and frustrations. We are all apt to think at the outset that human freedom means a man choosing what he wants to do at every hour of the day, and doing it. And superficially that is what freedom is. But just try. If you enjoy your freedom say on Monday and then again on Tuesday by the time Thursday comes it may turn out that something you greatly desired to be doing, longed to be doing from the bottom of your heart, you find that you just can't get on with it because your faculties have been so disorganised and divided by the superficial freedom you have been enjoying earlier in the week. And I think you see that at that time religion comes into freedom, don't you.?" ....

"You got freedom up to a point by having democratic institutions. Democratic institutions are a glorious thing given to us in the service of freedom. You don't secure freedom merely by having democratic institutions and enjoy them at will. You can have democratic institutions and yet the people can be enslaved to passions and prejudices and follies both the whole community or this group or that group. And if a country is truely free something else is needed beyond the possession of democratic institutions, namely the spirit of the citizens who operate them".

Breadth- "get on with your own subject, work at it hard, but do for Gods' sake be sure to take a little interest in other peoples subject. We all suffer so much from being specialised and not knowing at all about other person's craft or study. And that makes us narrow and un- imaginative.

Wonder:- "There are two sorts of educated men and the contrast between them is very big. A, a person academically stuffed right to the throat- boring and dull, B, too have successful academic carrier but is quite different. The effect on him is to make him full of wonder, wonder. My word, how wonderful is this knowledge!. How wonderful is the world with a vista of things. This sense of wonder keeps him humble, imaginative, alive and interesting and always looking beyond.........The sense of wonder at the world "O Lord, how wonderful art thy works" said the psalmist "I am fearfully and wonderfully made". If only education led every pupil at wonder at himself in just that way. "I thank thee O God for I am fearfully and wonderfully made". And then not only wonder at the world and wonder at yourself, but wonder also at the world's creator and the Father of all. "My God how wonderful Thou art."

Mother Teresa's address of the College Convocation on the 11th of March 1978 is another landmark occasion. Her simplicity in every aspect, approach to life and the content of the matter, touched each one present on the occasion. Only few could leave the convocation Pandal without tears in their eyes. She started "let us say a prayer for our young people in gratitude for what God has done for them during these years of training: May God bless and keep you, and be with you and guide you and lead you, and lead you in the right path; be a light to you; be a joy to you; be a strength to you; and let the joy of the Lord be your strength and bond of love, unity and peace".

"Looking at you our young people, I was thinking that it is as if a ticket has been given to you to walk out into the world. But there is a purpose in giving this going. You have worked all these years to be able today to stand up and be sent. We read in our scriptures that God loved the world so much that He gave His Son Jesus to be his love, his compassion in the world. And today this College, and the almighty God himself through this College sending you out to be His love, His compassion, to be the carriers of Gods' peace. For today the world is being torn apart for want of love, for want of understanding love, and you young people who have received so much love, and you young people who have received so much understanding love, be sure that it has been given to you, not to keep it for yourselves but to use it for others. There are thousands and thousands of young people of your age who haven't got what you have received, who have got in your own homes, and that is why today when you go out, you must see that whatever diploma you are receiving is not just a piece of paper, but is life. Let it be a torch in your own hands, a torch of love of life for those who are in darkness, for those who are hungry for love, for those who do not know what it is to be loved, for what it is to know human touch, for what it is to have somebody as your own. And here in the world today there are people who have forgotten what it is to be loved, who have forgotten that they also are capable of love"

....

"This is what you and I must be to our people, for they like you and me have been created for greater things. They have been created by the same loving hand of God to love and to be loved. So here in Agra find out where your poor people are. There are many people who need your tender hand, who need your understanding love. Let us not think that poor people, just because they are poor, are good for nothing. They are very great people, they are very lovable people" She gave examples and concluded "Love begins at home. If you want to love the poor with greater love begin loving at home, for no place is there for better practice than our home, and there is no better way of showing our love for God than by loving our neighbours. For Saint John writes in his epistle "you are a liar if you say that you love God whom you do not see, when you don't love your neighbour whom you do see"

"So today I ask one thing from you young people. Pray. Don't face the world without prayer, ask God to be your strength, your light, your love to be your purity. Only the pure heart can see God. Go with Him, put your hand in his hand. For he has called you by his name, he has guided you, he has looked after you. He has given you parents to look after you. He has given you parents to take care of you.

And you have been wanted. For today many children are not wanted. Abortion is nothing but being unwanted. And you have been wanted by your parents. So you owe your parents a deep gratitude, and best gratitude to show your parents is to be what they want you to be- a child of God, a carrier of God's love and compassion, a light in the darkness of this world. And my prayer for you will be that you are the future of our country, that it is you who will make it beautiful or ugly. I am sure that what you have received in this College is very beautiful. Make something beautiful for God."

Appendix (i)

<u>Chairpersons of Governing Bodies 1930-1999</u>
<u>Presiding Bishops</u>

Rt.Rev. Clarks John Godfrey Saunders
3rdBishop of Lucknow   **1928-1938**

Rt Rev. Sydney James Gossagel
4th Bishop of Lucknow   **1939-1947**

Rt.Rev.Chrystopher Robinson
5th Bishop of Lucknow   **1947-1962**

Rt.Rev. Joseph Amritanand
6th Bishop of Lucknow   **1962-1970**

Rt.Rev Din Dayal
7th Bishop of Lucknow   **1970-1976**

Rt.Rev. A.V. Joanathan
1st Bishop of Agra   **1976-1982**

Rt.Rev. W.O.Simon
2nd Bishop of Agra   **1982-1992**

Rt.Rev. Morris Andrews
3rd Bishop of Agra   **1992-1999**

Appendix (ii)

Vice-Principals of the College from
1930-1999

Rev. Canon T.D. Sully

Dr. C.V. Mahajhan

Canon Dr. P.T. Chandi

Canon N. Timothy

Prof. C.T. Gideon (Officiating Principal)

Dr. P.I. Itteyerah

Prof. M.A. Hakim

Prof. G.I. David (Officiating Principal)

Dr. M.S. Renick

Dr. Job Saffir

Dr. O.A.K. Das

Dr. Mrs. Agnes S. Ipe (Officiating Principal)

Late Prof. C. T. Gideon

Prof. C.T. Gideon

Dr. O.A. K. Das

Prof. G. I. David

Dr. Mrs. Agnes S.Ipe

Printed in the United States
By Bookmasters